Trotskyism
after Trotsky

The origins of the
International Socialists

Trotskyism after Trotsky

The origins of the International Socialists

Tony Cliff

BOOKMARKS

London, Chicago and Sydney

Trotskyism after Trotsky – Tony Cliff
First published 1999
Bookmarks Publications Ltd, 1 Bloomsbury Street, London WC1B 3QE,
England
Bookmarks, PO Box 16085, Chicago, Illinois 60616, USA
Bookmarks, PO Box A338, Sydney South, NSW 2000, Australia
Copyright © Bookmarks Publications Ltd

ISBN 1 898876 43 6

Printed by Larkham P&P
Cover by Sherborne Design

**Bookmarks Publications Ltd is linked to an international grouping of
socialist organisations:**
- **Australia:** International Socialist Organisation, PO Box A338, Sydney
  South
- **Britain:** Socialist Workers Party, PO Box 82, London E3 3LH
- **Canada:** International Socialists, PO Box 339, Station E, Toronto, Ontario
  M6H 4E3
- **Cyprus:** Ergatiki Demokratia, PO Box 7280, Nicosia
- **Denmark:** Internationale Socialister, Postboks 642, 2200 København N
- **Germany:** Linksruck, Postfach 304 183, 20359 Hamburg
- **Greece:** Socialistiko Ergatiko Komma, c/o Workers Solidarity, PO Box
  8161, Athens 100 10
- **Holland:** Internationale Socialisten, PO Box 92025, 1090AA Amsterdam
- **Ireland:** Socialist Workers Party, PO Box 1648, Dublin 8
- **New Zealand:** Socialist Workers Organisation, PO Box 8851, Auckland
- **Norway:** Internasjonale Socialisterr, Postboks 9226 Grønland, 0134 Oslo
- **Poland:** Solidarność Socjalistyczna, PO Box 12, 01-900 Warszawa 118
- **Spain:** Socialismo Internacional, Apartado 563, 08080 Barcelona
- **United States:** International Socialist Organization, PO Box 16085,
  Chicago, Illinois 60616
- **Zimbabwe:** International Socialist Organisation, PO Box 6758, Harare

Contents

Acknowledgements

Several people have helped in the writing of this book. Ian Birchall, Rob Ferguson, Al Richardson and the Socialist Platform Archive helped to locate documents of the Trotskyist movement for the years 1946-47. Many thanks are due to Chris Bambery, Alex Callinicos, Lindsey German, Chris Harman and John Rees for advice and suggestions. Chanie Rosenberg deserves a special thanks for participating in the editing of the manuscript and typing it. Thanks are also due to Donny Gluckstein for expert critical comments and many valuable stylistic suggestions, and to Rob Hoveman for very efficiently seeing the book through to publication.

Chapter 1

Recognising the problem

In *The Communist Manifesto* Marx and Engels argue that communists generalise from the historical and international experience of the working class. This experience is always changing and developing and therefore Marxism always changes; the moment Marxism stops changing, it is dead. Sometimes historical change happens slowly and almost imperceptibly, but sometimes the changes are radical. Consequently there are abrupt turning points in the history of Marxism.

For example, one cannot understand the breakthrough marked by the appearance of *The Communist Manifesto* without taking into account the background of the coming 1848 revolution.

Another turning point was the Paris Commune in 1871 which inspired Marx to write in *The Civil War in France*, 'The working class cannot take the old state machine to use it to build socialism'.[1] He argued that the working class must smash the capitalist state machine and build a new state without a police force, a standing army or a bureaucracy, a state in which all officials should be elected, instantly recallable and should get the same wages as the workers they represent. *The Communist Manifesto* had not mentioned any of this. Now Marx recognised the central features of a workers' state. He did not reach these conclusions from studying hard in the British Museum. His understanding flowed from the actions of Parisian workers who took power for 74 days and showed what kind of state the working class could establish.

Again, Trotsky's theory of permanent revolution was a by-product of the Russian Revolution of 1905. This theory argued that in backward and underdeveloped countries the bourgeoisie, being a latecomer, was too cowardly and conservative to solve bourgeois democratic tasks, such as winning national independence and agrarian reform. These tasks could be accomplished by revolution led by the working class at the head of the peasantry. In the process of solving these issues a workers' revolution would transcend the boundaries of bourgeois property norms and this would lead to the establishment of a workers' state.

The idea that the bourgeoisie was counter-revolutionary and that the working class would lead the peasantry were not insights which arose automatically from Trotsky's brilliant mind; they were discovered in reality in the 1905 revolution. This demonstrated in practice how the workers, not the bourgeoisie, struggled to overthrow Tsarism to exercise democratic control over society. Petrograd, at the centre of the revolution, even developed organs of a workers' state—workers' councils, or soviets. Further developments in Marxism by figures such as Lenin and Luxemburg also grew out of historical experience such as the latter's brilliant book about the mass strike, a by-product of struggles in Russia and Poland during 1905.

A new turning point occurred when Stalin attempted to wipe out the tradition of the Bolshevik Revolution. It fell to Trotsky to champion its defence. Until his murder in 1940 he did this brilliantly. However, at the end of the Second World War the Fourth International that he founded faced a new and decisive challenge—how to react to a situation radically different to that visualised by its founder. This created special difficulties because the movement had been deprived of the intellectual giant who had led it hitherto.

Trotsky's prognoses

Before his death Trotsky had made a series of predictions. Four of these would be challenged by the reality of developments after the Second World War.

(1) He had predicted that the Stalinist regime in Russia could

not survive the war. Thus, in an article on 1 February 1935, 'The Workers' State, Thermidor and Bonapartism', Trotsky argued that Stalinism, as a form of Bonapartism, 'cannot long maintain itself; a sphere balanced on the point of a pyramid must invariably roll down on one side or the other'; hence 'the inevitable collapse of the Stalinist regime' would follow.[2]

One outcome might be capitalist restoration. In the thesis 'War and the Fourth International' (10 June 1934) Trotsky wrote that 'in the case of a protracted war accompanied by the passivity of the world proletariat, the internal social contradictions in the USSR not only might lead but also have to lead to a bourgeois Bonapartist counter-revolution'.[3]

On 8 July 1936 he put forward an alternative scenario:

> The USSR will be able to emerge from a war without a defeat only under one condition, and that is if it is assisted by the revolution in the West or in the East. But the international revolution, the only way of saving the USSR, will at the same time be the death blow for the Soviet bureaucracy.[4]

Whichever perspective is considered, it is clear Trotsky was convinced of the instability of the Stalinist regime, so much so that on 25 September 1939, in an article, 'The USSR in War', he wrote that to see the Russian regime as a stable class system would be 'to place ourselves in a ludicrous position' because at that time it was 'just a few years or even a few months prior to its inglorious downfall'.[5]

The actual reality at the end of the Second World War was very different. The Stalinist regime did not collapse. As a matter of fact, after 1945 it went from strength to strength by expanding into Eastern Europe.

(2) Trotsky thought that capitalism was in terminal crisis. As a result production could not expand and, associated with this, there could be no serious social reforms or a rise in the masses' living standards. In 1938, in *The Death Agony of Capitalism and the Tasks of the Fourth International*, Trotsky wrote that the Western world was:

> ...in an epoch of decaying capitalism: when, in general, there can be no discussion of systematic social reforms and the raising of the masses' living standards...when every serious demand

of the proletariat and even every serious demand of the petty bourgeoisie inevitably reaches beyond the limits of capitalist property relations and of the bourgeois state.[6]

However, post-war world capitalism was not trapped in general stagnation and decay. Indeed, Western capitalism enjoyed a massive expansion and alongside this came a flourishing of reformism. As Mike Kidron pointed out, 'The system as a whole has never grown so fast for so long as since the war—twice as fast between 1950 and 1964 as between 1913 and 1950, and nearly half as fast again as during the generation before that'.[7]

In consequence the social democratic and Communist parties, far from disintegrating, emerged in the post-war period stronger in number and support than ever before. Reformism flourished on the basis of a rising standard of living.

In Britain, for example, the Attlee government represented the zenith of reformism. Formed in 1945, it was not only the first majority Labour government, it represented the high point of Labour Party history. Whatever the myths regarding the Labour government of 1945-51 there is no doubt that it was the most effective reformist Labour government of them all.

Under Attlee workers and their families fared much better than before the war. The government kept up a high level of expenditure on the social services; while food subsidies were pegged in the April 1949 budget at £465 million, they still represented a formidable sum and did much to keep down the cost of living for working people. And, of course, full employment and relatively mild inflation were immeasurable boons to workers.

One factor ensuring mass support for the government was full employment. Throughout Labour's tenure of office unemployment was extremely low (except during the fuel crisis of winter 1947 when it reached 3 percent). There were three and a half million more workers employed in June 1951 than six years previously.[8] Another factor was the welfare state whose flagship was the National Health Service.

The Labour Party's popularity with workers remained high. In 43 by-elections it lost only one seat! Furthermore the October 1951 general election gave Labour the highest poll ever achieved by one party—13,948,605 votes, 49.8 percent of the total votes cast. Only the vagaries of the electoral system gave the Tories a majority in parliament. Notwithstanding austerity and rationing at home, and wars overseas, Labour kept its support.[9]

And Britain was not the exception. Throughout Europe the standard of living improved. Full employment, or near full employment, prevailed. Systematic reforms were achieved and mass reformist parties did not wither away. In Germany, France, Spain, Norway, Sweden, Denmark and other countries, social democratic parties ruled for a long time.

(3) Using his theory of permanent revolution, Trotsky argued that in backward, underdeveloped countries the accomplishment of bourgeois democratic tasks—national liberation and agrarian reform—could be advanced only by working class power.

This too was refuted by actual events. In China, the most populous country in the world, Mao led a Stalinist party entirely divorced from the working class to unify the country, win independence from imperialism and institute land reforms. Similar processes occurred elsewhere such as in Cuba and Vietnam.

(4) Finally, if all the above three prognoses had been correct, there would not have been a future for Stalinism or reformism and the field would have been wide open for an extremely rapid advance of the Fourth International. On these grounds Trotsky was very confident that it had a great future in the coming few years.

On 10 October 1938 he wrote:

> Mankind has become poorer than it was 25 years ago, while the means of destruction have become infinitely more powerful. In the very first months of the war, therefore, a stormy reaction against the fumes of chauvinism will set in among the working masses. The first victims of this reaction, along with fascism, will be the parties of the Second and Third Internationals. Their collapse will be the indispensable condition for an avowed revolutionary movement, which will find for its crystallisation no axis other than the Fourth International. Its tempered cadres will lead the toilers to the great offensive.[10]

Trotsky had already stated that:

> When the centennial of *The Communist Manifesto* [ie 1948] is celebrated, the Fourth International will have become the decisive revolutionary force on our planet.[11]

On 18 October 1938, in a speech entitled 'The Founding of the Fourth International', Trotsky underlined the point:

> Ten years! Only ten years! Permit me to finish with a prediction: during the next ten years the programme of the Fourth International will become the guide of millions and these revolutionary millions will know how to storm earth and heaven.[12]

Repeated comments on the same theme establish the fact that his statements on the speedy victory of the Fourth International were not throwaway remarks, but were a constant thread until his death.

Alas, this prediction too was unfounded because his prognoses regarding Russia, Western capitalism and the Third World were belied by the actual reality of the events after 1945. Very little space remained for the Fourth International— the Trotskyist organisations remained minuscule with very little influence in the working class.

Trotsky's place in Marxism

A preliminary remark is necessary about the way we Trotskyists should look upon Trotsky. He was a political giant among us: the organiser of the October Revolution, the leader of the Red Army, the leader, with Lenin, of the Communist International.

Again and again, in dealing with the situation in Britain in 1926, or the Chinese Revolution of 1925-27, or Germany at the time of the rise of Nazism, France 1936 and Spain 1931-38, Trotsky demonstrated a fantastic ability to analyse complex situations, to prognosticate about future developments, and to suggest the strategy needed.

Trotsky's words were often prophetic. In many respects his analyses brilliantly stood the test of time. No one among the great Marxist thinkers surpassed him in the ability to use the historical materialist method, to synthesise economic, social and political factors, to see their inter-relationship with the mass psychology of millions, and grasp the import of the subjective factor—the role of workers' parties and workers' leaders in the great events.[13] Trotsky's *History of the Russian Revolution* towers over any other Marxist writing of history. It is an analytical and artistic monument of unprecedented richness and beauty.[14]

Trotsky's writings of the years 1928-40—the articles, essays and books on developments in Germany, France and Spain—are among the most brilliant Marxist writings. They are in the same league as the best historical writings of Karl Marx: *The Eighteenth Brumaire of Louis Bonaparte* and *The Class Struggles in France*. Trotsky did not limit himself to analysing situations but also put forward a clear line of action for the proletariat. In terms of strategy and tactics his writings are extremely valuable revolutionary manuals, comparable to the best produced by Lenin.

One example of a precious gem in Trotsky's works is his writings on Germany in the years preceding Hitler's rise to power. Germany was the country with the most important working class movement in the world at the time. It was entering a deep slump and social crisis, which was the background to the rapid growth of the Nazi movement. Faced with this, Trotsky brought to bear all his energy and knowledge. In this period he wrote innumerable short books, pamphlets and articles analysing the German situation. They are among the most brilliant pieces of writing he penned. Such prescience on the course of events is found nowhere else. He warned of the catastrophe threatening not only the German but also the international working class that would follow the rise of the Nazis. His call for action to stop them, for a united front of all labour movement organisations, became more and more urgent. Tragically his prophetic warnings and urgent calls were not heeded. His voice was a cry in the wilderness. Neither the Communist Party (KPD) nor the Social Democratic Party (SPD) paid any heed. If Trotsky's analysis and proposals for action had been accepted, the subsequent history of the century would have been completely different. Trotsky's analysis of German events was particularly impressive in view of the fact that the author was removed from the scene of the events by a considerable distance. Still he managed to follow the day to day twists and turns. Reading Trotsky's writings of the years 1930-33, their concreteness gives the clear impression that the author must have been living in Germany, not far away on the island of Prinkipo in Turkey.[15]

In the terrible dark days of the 1930s Trotsky shone for us as a brilliant guiding star. With the Nazis' terrifying advance and the Moscow show trials that condemned the leaders of the October Revolution, the Bolshevik Party and the Comintern as Nazi agents, our dependence ideologically and emotionally was deep and understandable. We were quite convinced, and rightly, of the genius of his analysis of the total situation and of the strategy and tactics needed to face it that he developed.

How did the Trotskyists come to terms with the situation after the Second World War?

After the war it was really excruciatingly painful to face the reality that Trotsky's prognoses regarding the future of the Stalinist regime and the economic, social and political situation in the capitalist West as well as in the backward and developing East did not come true. To repeat Trotsky's words literally while avoiding facing the real situation was to give too much honour to Trotsky, but also too much insult. It was to treat Trotsky as a supra-historical person; that fits a religious sect but not the disciples of scientific socialism, of Marxism. With a heavy heart we have to remember the saying ascribed to Aristotle: 'Plato is dear to me, but dearer still is truth.'

Understandably, but wrongly, the leadership of the Fourth International by and large refused to face the fact that key prognoses had been refuted by events. Facing this truth was a precondition for answering the question: why did they not come true? Asking the correct question is 90 percent of finding the answer. Long before Isaac Newton, apples used to fall off trees. His asking the question 'Why?' led to the law of gravity.

To overcome the crisis in world Trotskyism, one had to face the abyss between Trotsky's prognoses and reality. This did not necessarily happen.

Take Trotsky's first prediction. As quoted above, he thought

14

the Stalinist regime would not survive the war. Yet when Stalin continued to control Russia the conclusion of James P Cannon, leader of the Trotskyists in the United States, was that the war had therefore not ended!

> Trotsky predicted that the fate of the Soviet Union would be decided in the war. That remains our firm conviction. Only we disagree with some people who carelessly think the war is over. The war has only passed through one stage and is now in the process of regroupment and reorganisation for the second. The war is not over, and the revolution which we said would issue from the war in Europe is not taken off the agenda. It has only been delayed and postponed, primarily for lack of a sufficiently strong revolutionary party.[16]

This was an extreme case of scholasticism. In medieval times the scholastics, debating whether oil freezes in winter, did not apply a simple test—putting a container of oil in the snow and watching it—but looked for a quotation from Aristotle on the subject.

Eleven months after the end of the war it became clear even to the most blinkered Trotskyist that the Stalinist regime had survived the war. But still they insisted that the regime was in a very shaky condition. Thus the *Fourth International* of April 1946 stated:

> Without any fear of exaggeration, one can say that the Kremlin has never confronted a more critical situation at home and abroad than it does today.[17]

To support this assertion, the following anecdote was employed:

> ...there is the incident at a mass meeting addressed by Kalinin where a woman rose up to demand why he was wearing such fine polished boots while the masses had to walk barefoot or in bast shoes. This was indeed audacious! It indicates the degree to which the resentment among the masses against bureaucratic privileges has grown.[18]

However, far from depicting the parlous state of post-war Russia, as I told Ernest Mandel, a leading member of the Fourth International, when I met him in September 1946 in Paris, this story had been published many years before. Indeed, it referred to an incident that had happened more than a quarter of a century previously!

Nevertheless the conference of the Fourth International in April 1946 continued to assert that:

> Behind the appearance of power never before attained, there lurks the reality that the USSR and the Soviet bureaucracy have entered the critical phase of their existence.[19]

Trotsky's prediction of Stalinist collapse was the inescapable consequence of his analysis of the class character of Russia. If the prediction was wrong then his original analysis necessarily fell into question. If so a new explanation of the Stalinist bureaucracy was necessary. One way of approaching this task was to ask what the class nature was of the countries of Eastern Europe taken over by Stalin, countries soon remodelled as almost exact replicas of Russia itself.

The Fourth International completely accepted Trotsky's view that Russia was a workers' state, a 'degenerated workers' state', a workers' state distorted by a ruling bureaucracy. Yet if Poland, Czechoslovakia, Hungary, etc had the same nature as Russia, then did it not follow that Stalin had brought about a revolution in Eastern Europe? Was he not therefore a revolutionary rather than a counter-revolutionary? That would not do. At first the leaders of the Fourth International solved the contradiction very simply: despite the similarities between them, the Eastern bloc countries were still capitalist countries, while Russia was a workers' state.

Mandel stated in September 1946 that 'all the People's Democracies', Yugoslavia included, were capitalist countries. Stalinists did not bring about a revolution in Eastern Europe, but a counter-revolution. To quote only what he wrote about Yugoslavia and Albania: 'In these two countries, the Soviet bureaucracy did not have to carry on any consistent counter-revolutionary activity; the native Stalinists took this upon themselves.' In both countries the Stalinists had constructed 'a new bourgeois state apparatus'.[20]

For a further two years the Fourth International continued with the same line regarding Eastern Europe. The resolution of the Second World Congress of the Fourth International, April 1948, says on the class nature of the 'People's Democracies'

(Yugoslavia included) that 'these countries retain their fundamentally capitalist structure... Thus, while maintaining bourgeois function and structure, the state of the "buffer" countries represents at the same time an extreme form of Bonapartism.' It continued, 'The "People's Democracies" are capitalist countries with "extreme forms of Bonapartism", "police dictatorships", etc. Therefore, the destruction of capitalism could be carried out only by the "revolutionary action of the masses" which was not yet a fact since a revolution demands the violent destruction of the bureaucratic state machine.' Thus you could not defend any of these states but had to observe the 'strictest revolutionary defeatism'.[21]

Two months later, when Tito broke with Stalin, the Fourth International did a somersault: Yugoslavia was not a capitalist country under a police-Bonapartist dictatorship any more, but an authentic workers' state. On 1 July 1948 the International Secretariat of the Fourth International issued an 'Open Letter to the Communist Party of Yugoslavia': 'You hold in your hands a mighty power if only you persevere on the road of socialist revolution', and noted in conclusion 'the promise of victorious resistance by a revolutionary workers' party against the Kremlin machine... Long live the Yugoslav Socialist Revolution'.[22] This was as shallow an analysis as the first position and ignored Tito's boast to the Fifth Congress of the Communist Party of Yugoslavia in 1948 that he and his friends knew how to tackle 'Trotskyist-fascists' by bringing them before the People's Courts and making them pay the supreme penalty. As *Borba* of 4 July 1948 put it:

> A handful of Trotskyists, who showed their true faces in the war as collaborators and agents of the invaders, ended shamefully before the People's Courts.[23]

With flip-flops like this taking place so easily, Michel Pablo, general secretary of the Fourth International, carried the new line that Russia's Eastern bloc were types of workers' states to the extreme. In 1949 he introduced the notion of 'centuries of deformed workers' states'.[24] In April 1954 Pablo wrote, 'Caught between the imperialist threat and the World Revolution, the Soviet bureaucracy aligned itself with the World Revolution'.[25] Furthermore the Soviet bureaucracy was carrying, and would continue to carry, the de-bureaucratisation and 'total and actual liberalisation of the regime'.[26] Pablo became an apologist for Stalinism. If there were going to be 'centuries of deformed workers' states' what role was there for Trotskyism or workers' revolution? Stalinism was made to appear progressive and Trotskyism irrelevant.

Going further than Pablo in baptising different countries as workers' states was Julian Posadas, the Argentinian Trotskyist and leader of one version of the Fourth International. In addition to the East European countries, Cuba, China, North Vietnam, North Korea and Outer Mongolia, Posadas discovered that a whole number of other countries were workers' states. Posadas declared:

> ...the International must follow closely the evolution of a series of countries of Africa [and] Asia, which are developing into workers' states, such as Syria, Egypt, Iraq, Mali, Guinea, Congo Brazzaville, etc, to determine when they pass into being workers' states.[27]

Perversely, Posadas looked forward with enthusiasm to a world atomic war. He called on the Soviet Union to nuke the United States. An 'Extraordinary Conference' of his Fourth International in 1962 declared:

> ...atomic war is inevitable. It will destroy perhaps half of humanity; it is going to destroy immense human riches. It is very possible. The atomic war is going to provoke a true inferno on earth. But it will not impede communism. Communism is an achieved necessity, not because of the material goods produced, but because it is in the consciousness of human beings. When humanity reacts and works in a communist form as it is working [sic], there is no atomic bomb capable of turning back that which human consciousness has acquired and learned...
>
> History, in its violent, spasmodic form, is demonstrating that little time remains for capitalism. Little time. We can say in a completely conscientious and certain way that if the workers' states fulfil their historical duty of aiding the colonial revolutions, capitalism doesn't have ten years of life. This is an audacious declaration but it is totally logical. Capitalism hasn't ten years of life. If the workers' states launch support of the colonial revolution with all their forces, capitalism has not five years of life, and the atomic war will last a very short time.[28]

Half humanity will be eliminated! But that does not matter: the victory of communism is assured!

> We are preparing ourselves for a stage in which before the atomic war we shall struggle for power, during the atomic war we shall struggle for power and we shall be in power, and immediately after the atomic war we shall be in power. There is no beginning, there is an end to atomic war, because atomic war is simultaneous revolution in the whole world; not as a chain reaction, simultaneous. Simultaneity doesn't mean the same day and the same hour. Great historic events should not be measured by hours or days, but by periods... The working class alone will maintain itself, will immediately have to seek its cohesion and centralisation...
>
> After destruction commences, the masses are going to emerge in all countries—in a short time, in a few hours. Capitalism cannot defend itself in an atomic war except by putting itself in caves and attempting to destroy all that it can. The masses, in contrast, are going to come out, will have to come out, because it is the only way to survive, defeating the enemy... The apparatus of capitalism, police, army, will not be able to resist... It will be necessary to organise the workers' power immediately...[29]

By this logic, if an H-bomb fell on London, the remnants of the working class, paralysed by fear and impotence, would take power! Thus Marxism turns from a shibboleth into a talisman! From workers' states in which workers have no power, no say, to workers' revolution as a result of the atomic destruction of workers! What ideological retrogression. In the 19th century Utopian Socialism was superseded by scientific socialism—Marxism—but now Marxism was being replaced by 'miracle' socialism!

Mandel, Pablo and Posadas came from the same stable—dogmatic Trotskyism that stuck to the words of Trotsky while emptying them of their spirit.

What about Trotsky's second prognosis involving the fate of world capitalism? In the face of a developing boom which would be the longest in capitalism's history, the Fourth International conference of April 1946 declared:

> ...there is no reason whatsoever to assume that we are facing

a new epoch of capitalist stabilisation and development... The war has aggravated the disorganisation of capitalist economy and has destroyed the last possibilities of a relatively stable equilibrium in social and international relations.[30]

Furthermore:

The revival of economic activity in capitalist countries weakened by the war, and in particular continental European countries, will be characterised by an especially slow tempo which will keep their economy at levels bordering on stagnation and decay.[31]

It was admitted that 'the American economy will soon experience a relative boom...' but this boom would be short lived: 'The United States will then head for a new economic crisis which will be more deep-going and widespread than that of 1929-33, with far more devastating repercussions on world economy.' The prospects for British capitalism were 'a lengthy period of grave economic difficulties, convulsions, and partial and general crises'. What would be the condition of workers throughout the world? 'The proletariat [will] continue to work under far worse living conditions than those existing before the war'.[32]

A rising revolutionary wave was inevitable under these conditions because of:

...the resistance of the proletariat, demanding an improvement in its living conditions, an improvement which is incompatible with the possibility of reviving capitalism.

If the war did not immediately create in Europe a revolutionary upsurge of the scope and tempo we anticipated, it is nonetheless undeniable that it destroyed capitalist equilibrium on a world scale, thus opening up a long revolutionary period...[33]

The stagnation of world capitalism and mass unemployment would generate a general revolutionary situation:

What confronts us now is a worldwide crisis transcending anything known in the past, and a worldwide revolutionary upsurge developing, to be sure, at unequal tempos in different parts of the world, but unceasingly exercising reciprocal influence from one centre to another, and thus determining a long revolutionary perspective.[34]

In 1946 the Fourth International predicted that the revolutionary wave would be much broader and higher than that which followed the First World War:

> Following World War One, the graph of revolutionary struggle was characterised at the outset by a brief and precipitate rise, which attained its peak by the spring of 1919, and was followed by a sharp and continuous decline, interrupted only by a new and very brief upswing in 1923.
>
> This time the graph of revolutionary struggle begins with a slow and hesitant rise, interrupted by many oscillations or partial retreats, but its general tendency is upwards. The importance of this fact is obvious. While the post World War One movement suffered at the very beginning from the burden of initial defeats, above all in Germany, the present movement, on the contrary, suffers from the fact that at no time as yet have the full forces of the proletariat been thrown into battle. The defeats, therefore, are transient and relative in character, do not jeopardise the subsequent developments of events, and can be neutralised by the passage of the struggle to a more advanced stage.[35]

The only other alternative envisaged was that, if the revolutionary wave did not lead to proletarian victory, bourgeois democracy would be replaced in a very short time by new fascist regimes:

> From the moment that it acquires its own repressive apparatus again, and the economic and social conditions threaten the existence of its system, the big bourgeoisie will answer every action of the proletarian masses with merely larger and larger financial contributions to the neo-fascist 'leaders'. Their sole difficulty here will be one of choice; for if we study attentively the political situation in the various European countries, we find already, on the political scene, not one, but several figures who are potential Doriots, Mussolinis and Degrelles of tomorrow. In this sense the fascist danger already exists on the entire continent.[36]

In 1947 Mandel wrote an article which reached the following conclusions:

> ...the following [are] characteristics of the cycle of production under capitalist decadence:

(a) The crises last longer, are more violent, and carry a much longer stagnation than the period of revival and prosperity. Ascendant capitalism appeared as a long prosperity, interrupted by brief interludes of crisis. Decadent capitalism appears as a long crisis interrupted by revivals which are more and more unstable and brief.

(b) The world market ceases to expand globally. There is no more boom on a world scale. The splitting up of the world market or the violent destruction of a competitor alone allows for the development of feverish booms in certain capitalist countries.

(c) There is no more all round development of productive forces on a national scale. Even during the period of 'prosperity' certain branches develop only at the expense of other branches. Advances in technology are no longer or are only very partially incorporated in production.

(d) There is no more all round amelioration of the standard of living of the industrial workers from one revival to another. This naturally does not exclude either a relative 'amelioration' between the crisis and the revival, or a relative amelioration of the position of unemployed or peasants etc, transformed during the 'revival' into industrial workers.[37]

What a fantasy world!

Anybody reading today, for the first time, the above statements of Mandel, Pablo and Posadas and of the Fourth International must be shocked that rational human beings could carry such illusions. There is no one so blind as he who will not see. The leading members of the Trotskyist movement made enormous efforts to avoid looking at reality. In retrospect one cannot but be surprised. But to understand the refusal of the leading Trotskyists to confront reality one must understand how much pain this reality inflicted on them, shattering the grand hopes they had. The Trotskyist movement acted like the Christian sects in the 16th and 17th centuries who clung onto the old ideas of medieval times when that world was disintegrating and the new capitalist one was still being established. Their burning of witches was an irrational act, but it can be explained rationally.

However one understands the motives behind Mandel, Pablo

and Posadas, they cannot be justified. For Marxists, rule number one is, if you want to change reality, you must understand it. The disarray in the ranks of the Trotskyist movement, the zigzags, the splits, were an inevitable product of not grasping the real situation in which the working class found itself. They were trying to chart a course with a map that was hopelessly out of date. Thus world Trotskyism entered a cul-de-sac. The general crisis of the movement demanded a radical re-evaluation of the perspectives of humanity.

Preserving the essence of Trotskyism while deviating from the letter of Trotsky's words

The few comrades who started the International Socialist tendency were not prepared to use Marxism as a substitute for reality, but on the contrary wished it to be a weapon helping to master this reality. In the years 1946-48 we had to wrestle with very difficult questions. We had to be clear that we were continuing a tradition—that we were followers of Marx, Lenin and Trotsky—but that we had to face new situations. It was both a continuation and a new beginning. Intellectual toughness does not mean dogmatism; grasping a changing reality does not mean vagueness. Our criticism of orthodox Trotskyism was conceived as a return to classical Marxism.

The discussion which follows below will not approach the issues on the basis of hindsight. Hindsight vision is always perfect. We shall have to see how three theories evolved in reaction to events shortly after the end of the Second World War—the theories of state capitalism, the permanent arms economy and deflected permanent revolution. The three areas these dealt with—Russia and Eastern Europe, advanced capitalist countries, and the Third World—covered the whole globe.

Here each question will initially be treated as separate. Only later will it be possible to find their interconnections and thus explain the total pattern of development. Only standing on the top of a mountain and looking down can one see how the different paths converge.

Chapter 2

State capitalism

Why did the Stalinist regime survive? What was the nature of the 'People's Democracies' of Eastern Europe? What did their creation show about the nature of the Stalinist regime? The theory of state capitalism was developed out of the attempt to answer these questions. The answers defined Stalinist Russia as a state capitalist country.

The first document in which Russia was defined as state capitalist by the present author was a very long duplicated document of 142 pages written in 1948 and entitled 'The Class Nature of Stalinist Russia'. However, to understand the genesis of the theory it is useful to consider the 'People's Democracies', those countries overrun by the Russian army at the end of the Second World War. Napoleon said, 'Une armée dehors c'est l'état qui voyage' (an army abroad is but the state on the move), and this maxim applies very well to places like Poland and Hungary whose governments were nothing but extensions of the Russian state. Therefore, the study of these gave an insight into the regime of the 'mother country'.

Although it was through the prism of the 'People's Democracies' that one could see clearly the shape of Stalinist Russia, the argument was formulated in writing only after 'The Class Nature of Stalinist Russia' had appeared. In 1950 'On the Class Nature of the People's Democracies' was published. Its starting point was that if the Eastern European states were truly workers' states then a social revolution ought to have taken place there; conversely if no social revolution had occurred, then the nature of the East European states had to be re-evaluated.

The discussion was built around Marx and Lenin's theory of

the state. Marx frequently repeated the idea that the political supremacy of the working class is a prerequisite for its economic
supremacy. The workers cannot own the means of production
collectively—that is, be the ruling class economically—unless the
state which owns and controls the means of production is in their
hands; in other words, unless the proletariat has political power.

In this respect the proletariat is fundamentally different
from the bourgeoisie. The latter has direct ownership over
wealth; therefore, whatever the form of government, so long
as the bourgeoisie is not expropriated, it does not cease to
be the ruling class. A capitalist can own his property in a
feudal monarchy, in a bourgeois republic, in a fascist dictatorship, under military rule, under Robespierre, Hitler,
Churchill or Attlee. Against this workers are separated from
the means of production and it is this very fact which makes
them into wage slaves. If a situation arises where the state
is the repository of the means of production but is totally
alienated from the working class, they cannot be the ruling
class.[38]

A few quotations from the great Marxist thinkers illustrate
these points. *The Communist Manifesto* declares:

> ...the first step in the revolution by the working class is to raise
> the proletariat to the position of ruling class, to win the battle
> for democracy.
>
> The proletariat will use its political supremacy to wrest, by
> degrees, all capital from the bourgeoisie, to centralise all in-
> struments of production in the hands of the state, ie the pro-
> letariat organised as the ruling class...[39]

The proletarian revolution is the victory of 'the battle of
democracy'. The workers' state is 'the proletariat organised as
the ruling class'. How could a Stalinist 'social revolution' im-
posed by Red Army tanks entirely from outside fit the Marxist conception of the role of proletarian class consciousness in
the revolution?

Marx repeated hundreds of times that the proletarian revolution is the conscious act of the working class itself. Therefore, if we accepted that the 'People's Democracies' were
workers' states, what Marx and Engels said about the socialist revolution being 'history conscious of itself' was refuted.

The same would be true of Engels' statement:

> It is only from this point [the socialist revolution] that men, with full consciousness, will fashion their own history; it is only from this point that the social causes set in motion by men will have, predominantly and in constantly increasing measure, the effects willed by men. It is humanity's leap from the realm of necessity into the realm of freedom.[40]

Rosa Luxemburg, too, must have been wrong in her summing up of what all the Marxist teachers wrote about the place of proletarian consciousness in a revolution:

> In all the class struggles of the past, carried through in the interests of minorities, and in which, to use the words of Marx, 'all the development took place in opposition to the great masses of the people', one of the essential conditions of action was the ignorance of these masses with regard to the real aims of the struggle, its material content, and its limits. This discrepancy was, in fact, the specific historical basis of the 'leading role' of the 'enlightened' bourgeoisie, which corresponded with the role of the masses as docile followers. But, as Marx wrote as early as 1845, 'as the historical action deepens, the number of masses engaged in it must increase. The class struggle of the proletariat is the 'deepest' of all historical actions up to our day, it embraces the whole of the lower layers of the people, and, from the moment that society became divided into classes, it is the first movement which is in accordance with the real interests of the masses. That is why the enlightenment of the masses with regard to their tasks and methods is an indispensable historical condition for socialist action, just as in former periods the ignorance of the masses was the condition for the action of the dominant classes.[41]

Pablo and Mandel sought a way around this problem by talking of a 'Bismarckian path of development' of the proletarian revolution, comparing it to the way German capitalism grew under the political rule of the Kaiser's Chancellor and the old landowning group—the Junkers. These Trotskyists hoped to prove that the proletarian social revolution could be carried without the revolutionary action of the proletariat itself by a state bureaucracy with 'a momentum of its own'. This idea, if thought out, led to the most shocking conclusions. It is true that the bourgeoisie took power in many and various ways. As a matter of fact there was only one pure case in which they carried through to the end a revolutionary struggle against feudalism—this was in France after 1789. In the case of England they compromised with the feudal landowners. In Germany and Italy, Poland and Russia, China and South America, they came to power without a revolutionary struggle. In America the almost complete non-existence of feudal remnants enabled the bourgeoisie to avoid an anti-feudal revolutionary struggle.

The 'Bismarckian' path was not the exception for the bourgeoisie, but almost the rule. France was the exception. If the proletarian revolution is not necessarily achieved through the activity of the working class itself but by a state bureaucracy, then the Russian Revolution would inevitably be the exception, while the 'Bismarckian' path would be the rule. The conclusion would be that no independent revolutionary leadership (by Trotskyists) would be needed.

Moreover, the rise of the bourgeoisie was achieved by mobilising the masses and then deceiving them—whether in the case of the French *sans-culottes* or the soldiers of Bismarck. If a proletarian revolution can be carried out in this way the law of lesser resistance meant history would choose the path of revolution carried out by small minorities deceiving the big majorities.[42]

The document 'The Class Nature of the People's Democracies' ended by pointing out that although members of the Fourth International repeated the basic Marxist conceptions—the liberation of the working class can be carried out only by the working class itself, the workers cannot lay hold of the bourgeois state machine but must smash it and establish a new state based on proletarian democracy (soviets, etc)—they persisted in calling the 'People's Democracies' workers' states.

The reason for this lay in conceiving of Russia as a degenerated workers' state. If Russia was a workers' state even though the workers were separated from the means of production, had no say in running the economy and state, and were subordinated to the most monstrous bureaucratic and militarist state machine, there was no reason why workers' revolutions establishing new workers' states should not be carried out without the independent, class conscious activity of the working class, without the smashing of the existing bureaucratic and militarist state machines. It would have been enough for the bureaucracy to be able to expropriate the bourgeoisie while keeping the workers 'in their place' for the transition from capitalism to a workers' state to be accomplished.

If the Marxist-Leninist theory of revolution had been turned upside down when the 'People's Democracies' were regarded as some kind of workers' states, what about the nature of a workers' state itself?[43]

The starting point for an analysis of this issue was a critical examination of Trotsky's definition of Russia as a degenerated workers' state. Can a state not under workers' control be a workers' state?

In Trotsky's works we find two different and quite contradictory definitions of a workers' state. According to one, the criterion for a workers' state is whether the proletariat has direct or indirect control, no matter how restricted, over state power: that is, whether the proletariat can get rid of the bureaucracy by reform alone, without the need for revolution. In 1931 he wrote:

> The recognition of the present Soviet state as a workers' state not only signifies that the bourgeoisie can conquer power in no other way than by armed uprising but also that the proletariat of the USSR has not forfeited the possibility of submitting the bureaucracy to it, or reviving the party again and of mending the regime of the dictatorship, without a new revolution, with the methods and on the road of reform.[44]

Trotsky expressed this idea even more clearly in a letter probably written at the end of 1928 where he wrote in answer to the question, 'Is the degeneration of the apparatus and of the Soviet power a fact?'

> There is no doubt that the degeneration of the Soviet apparatus is considerably more advanced than the same process in the party apparatus. Nevertheless, it is the party that decides. At present, this means the party apparatus. The question thus comes down to the same thing: is the proletarian kernel of the party, assisted by the working class, capable of triumphing over the autocracy of the party apparatus which is fusing with the state

apparatus? Whoever replies in advance that it is incapable, thereby speaks not only of the necessity of a new party on a new foundation, but also of the necessity of a second and new proletarian revolution.[45]

Later in the same letter Trotsky says:

> If the party is a corpse, a new party must be built on a new spot, and the working class must be told about it openly. If Thermidor [the reactionary movement during the Great French Revolution which halted and set into reverse the process of revolution] is completed, and if the dictatorship of the proletariat is liquidated, the banner of the second proletarian revolution must be unfurled. That is how we would act if the road of reform, for which we stand, proved hopeless.[46]

Trotsky's second definition had a fundamentally different criterion. No matter how independent the state machine may be from the masses, and even if the only way of getting rid of the bureaucracy is by revolution, so long as the means of production are state owned, the state remains a workers' state with the proletariat the ruling class.

Three conclusions are to be drawn from this:

(a) Trotsky's second definition of the workers' state negates the first.

(b) If the second definition is correct, *The Communist Manifesto* was incorrect in saying that 'the first step in the revolution by the working class is to raise the proletariat to the position of the ruling class'. Furthermore, in this case, neither the Paris Commune nor the Bolshevik dictatorship were workers' states as the former did not statify the means of production at all, and the latter did not do so for some time.

(c) If the state is the repository of the means of production and the workers do not control it, they do not own the means of production—that is, they are not the ruling class. The first definition admits this, the second avoids this but does not disprove it.

Russia's definition as a workers' state and the Marxist theory of the state

The assumption that Russia was a degenerated workers' state led inevitably to conclusions in direct contradiction to the Marxist concept of the state. An analysis of the role of what Trotsky called political revolution and social counter-revolution will prove this.

During bourgeois political revolutions, for instance the French revolutions of 1830 and 1848, the form of government changed to a greater or lesser degree, but the type of state remained the same—'special bodies of armed men, prisons, etc', independent of the people and serving the capitalist class.

However, there is a necessarily much closer connection between content and form in a workers' state than in any other state. Therefore, even if we assume that political revolutions can take place in a workers' state, one thing is clear—the same workers' state machine must continue to exist after the proletarian political revolution as before. If Russia really was a workers' state, then if the workers' party carried out a large scale 'purge' in a political revolution, it could and would use the existing state machine. On the other hand, for the former bourgeoisie to be restored, it could not use the existing state machine, but would be compelled to smash it and build another on its ruins.

Were these conditions obtaining in Russia? To pose the question correctly goes half way to answering it. If the bourgeoisie came to power it could certainly use the KGB, the regular army and so on. It is surely evident that a revolutionary party could have used neither the KGB, nor the bureaucracy, nor the standing army. The revolutionary party would have had to smash the existing state and replace it with soviets, people's militia, etc.

Trotsky partially avoided applying the lessons of the Marxist theory of the state by saying that the revolutionary party would begin with the restoration of democracy in the trade unions and the soviets.[47] But actually there were neither trade unions nor soviets in Russia in which democracy could be restored. A workers' state would not be re-established by reforming the Stalinist state machine, but by smashing it and building a new one.

If the proletariat had to smash the existing state machine on coming to power, while the bourgeoisie could use it, Russia was not a workers' state. Even if we assume that both proletariat and bourgeoisie would have required a 'purgation of the state apparatus' (necessarily involving such a deep change as to transform it qualitatively), we must again conclude that Russia was not a workers' state.

To believe that the proletariat and the bourgeoisie could use the same state machine as the instrument of their supremacy was tantamount to a refutation of the revolutionary content of the theory of the state as expressed by Marx, Engels, Lenin and Trotsky himself.

The form of property considered independently of the relations of production—a metaphysical abstraction

One feature of Russia which Trotsky stressed proved it was a workers' state (even if degenerated) was the absence of large scale private property and the predominance of state property. However, it is an axiom of Marxism that to consider private property independently of the relations of production is to create a supra-historical abstraction.

Human history knows the private property of the slave system, the feudal system, the capitalist system, all of which are fundamentally different from one another. Marx ridiculed Proudhon's attempt to define private property independently of the relations of production:

> In each historical epoch, property has developed differently and under a set of entirely different social relations. Thus to define bourgeois property is nothing less than to give an exposition of all the social relations of bourgeois production. To try to give a definition of property as if an independent relation, a category apart—an abstract eternal idea—can be nothing but an illusion of metaphysics or jurisprudence.[48]

Capitalism as a system is the sum total of the relations of production. All the categories which express relations between people in the capitalist process of production—value, price, wages, etc—constitute an integral part of it. It was the laws of movement of the capitalist system which defined the character of capitalist private property in its historical context and differentiated it from other sorts of private property. Proudhon, who abstracted the form of property from the relations of production, 'entangled the whole of these economic relations [the capitalist relations of production] in the general juristic conception of "property".' Therefore, 'Proudhon could not get beyond the answer which Brissot, in a similar work, had already, before 1789, given in the same words: "Property is theft".'[49]

That one form of private property can have a different historical character to another, can be the stronghold of a different class than another, was made quite clear by Marx. That the same can also apply to statified property is not so evident. This is because history, in the main, witnessed the class struggle on the basis of private property. Cases of class differentiation not based on private property are not very numerous and, on the whole, not very well known. Nevertheless they have existed.

As an example, let us take a chapter from the history of Europe: the Catholic church in the Middle Ages. The church had tremendous tracts of land on which hundreds of thousands of peasants laboured. The relations between the church and the peasants were the same feudal relations as existed between the feudal manor owner and his peasants. The church as such was feudal. At the same time none of the bishops, cardinals, etc, had individual rights over feudal property. It was the relations of production which defined the feudal class character of the church property, notwithstanding the fact that it was not private.

The Russian bureaucracy—a gendarme who appears in the process of distribution?

Another feature of Trotsky's theory of Russia being a degenerated workers' state was that the Stalinist regime did not constitute a new ruling class. Instead it played the role of a bureaucracy, rather like that of the trade union leaders. He believed this had occurred because in Russia the scarcity of goods compelled purchasers to stand in a queue and the bureaucracy's function was that of a gendarme who controlled the queue.

Was this the case? Was the bureaucracy's function limited to the process of distribution, or did it appear in the process of production as a whole, of which the former was but a subordinate part? This issue is of enormous theoretical importance.

Before attempting to answer this question, let us examine what Marx thought about the connection between the relations of production and distribution. Marx wrote:

> To the single individual, distribution naturally appears as a law established by the society determining his position in the sphere of production, within which he produces, and thus antedating production. At the outset the individual has no capital, no landed property. From his birth he is assigned to wage labour by the social forces of distribution. But this very condition of being assigned to wage labour is the result of the existence of capital and landed property as independent agents of production.
>
> From the point of view of society as a whole, distribution seems to antedate and to determine production in another way as well, as a pre-economic fact, so to say. A conquering people divides the land among the conquerors establishing thereby a certain division and form of landed property and determining the character of production; or it turns the conquered people into slaves and thus makes slave labour the basis of production. Or a nation, by revolution, breaks up large estates into small parcels of land and by this new distribution imparts to production a new character. Or legislation perpetuates land ownership in large families or distributes labour as an hereditary privilege and thus fixes it in castes. In all of these cases, and they are all historic, it is not distribution that seems to be organised and determined by production, but on the contrary, production by distribution.
>
> In the most shallow conception of distribution, the latter appears as the distribution of products and to that extent as further removed from and quasi-independent of production. But before distribution means distribution of products, it is first a distribution of the means of production, and second, what is

practically another wording of the same fact, it is a distribution of the members of society among the various kinds of production (the subjection of individuals to certain conditions of production). The distribution of products is manifestly a result of this distribution, which is bound up with the process of production and determines the very organisation of the latter.[50]

This extract from Marx, the essence of which is repeated time and time again throughout his works, is sufficient as a point of departure for the analysis of the place of the Stalinist bureaucracy in the economy.

Did the bureaucracy only administer the distribution of means of consumption among the people, or did it also administer the distribution of the people in the process of production? Did the bureaucracy exercise a monopoly over the control of distribution only, or over the control of the means of production as well? Did it ration means of consumption only or did it also distribute the total labour time of society between accumulation and consumption, between the production of means of production and that of means of consumption? Did the relations of production prevailing in Russia not determine the relations of distribution which comprised a part of them? These questions are answered by looking at the historical record.

Stalinist Russia becomes state capitalist

Marx's analysis of capitalism involves a theory of the relations between the exploiters and the exploited, and among the exploiters themselves. The two main features of the capitalist mode of production are the separation of the workers from the means of production and the transformation of labour power into a commodity which the workers must sell in order to live, and the reinvestment of surplus value—the accumulation of capital—which is forced on the individual capitalists by their competitive struggle with one another. Both these features characterised the Soviet Union during the first Five Year Plan (1928-32). The collectivisation of agriculture in these years was closely analogous to the expropriation of the English peasantry—the enclosures which Marx analysed in *Capital* under the chapter 'Primitive Accumulation of Capital'. In both cases the direct producers were deprived of the land and were therefore forced to sell their labour power.

But was the Russian economy under pressure to accumulate capital? On this I wrote the following:

> The Stalinist state is in the same position vis-à-vis the total labour time of Russian society as a factory owner vis-à-vis the labour of his employees. In other words, the division of labour is planned. But what is it that determines the actual division of the total labour time of Russian society? If Russia had not to compete with other countries, this division would be absolutely arbitrary. But as it is, Stalin's decisions are based on factors outside his control, namely the world economy, world competition. From this point of view the Russian state is in a similar position to the owners of a single capitalist enterprise competing with other enterprises.
>
> The rate of exploitation, that is, the ratio between surplus value and wages (s/v) does not depend on the arbitrary will of the Stalinist government but is dictated by world capitalism. The same applies to improvements in technique, or, to use what is practically an equivalent phrase in Marxian terminology, the relation between constant and variable capital, that is, between machinery, building, materials, etc, on the one hand, and wages on the other (c/v). The same, therefore, applies to the division of the total labour time of Russian society between production of means of production and of means of consumption. Hence, when Russia is viewed within the international economy, the basic features of capitalism can be discerned: 'anarchy in the social division of labour and despotism in that of the workshop are mutual conditions the one of the other'.[51]

It was during the first Five Year Plan that the mode of production in the USSR turned capitalist. Now, for the first time, the bureaucracy sought to create a proletariat and to accumulate capital rapidly. In other words, it sought to complete the historical mission of the bourgeoisie as quickly as possible. A quick accumulation of capital on the basis of a low level of production, of a small national income per capita, put heavy pressure on the consumption of the masses and their standard of living. Under such conditions, the bureaucracy, transformed into a personification of capital, for whom the accumulation of capital is the be all and end all, had to eliminate all remnants of workers' control. It had to substitute conviction in the labour process with coercion, to atomise the working class, and to force all social-political life into a totalitarian mould.

It was obvious that the bureaucracy, in the process of accumulating capital and oppressing the workers, would not be tardy in making use of its social supremacy in the relations of production in order to gain advantages for itself in the relations of distribution. Thus industrialisation and technical revolution in agriculture ('collectivisation') in a backward country under conditions of siege transformed the bureaucracy, from a layer under the direct and indirect pressure and control of the proletariat, into a ruling class.

Dialectical historical development, full of contradictions and surprises, brought it about that the first step that the bureaucracy took with the subjective intention of hastening the building of 'socialism in one country' became the foundation of the building of state capitalism.[52]

During the first and second Five Year Plans consumption was completely subordinated to accumulation. Thus the share of consumer goods in total output fell from 67.2 percent in 1927-28 to 39.0 percent in 1940; over the same period the share of producer goods rose from 32.8 percent to 61.0 percent. This is in contrast to the period of 1921-28 when, despite the bureaucratic deformation, consumption was not subordinated to accumulation, but a more or less balanced growth of production, consumption and accumulation took place.

This analysis of Russia as bureaucratic state capitalist followed Trotsky's theory of permanent revolution in taking the capitalist world system as its basic frame of reference. If it is a step forward from Trotsky's analysis of the Stalinist regime as given in *The Revolution Betrayed* and elsewhere, it is that it tried to take account of the pressure of world capitalism on the mode of production and the relations of production prevailing in the USSR. Trotsky's explanation did not reveal the dynamic of the system; it restricted itself to forms of property instead of dealing with the relations of production. It did not supply a political economy of the system. The theory of bureaucratic state capitalism tries to do both.

But let us be clear that only by standing on the shoulders of the giant, Leon Trotsky, with his theory of permanent revolution, his opposition to the doctrine of 'socialism in one country', and his heroic struggle against the Stalinist bureaucracy, could one have any comprehension of the Stalinist order.

It was the opportunity of looking at the Stalinist regime years after Trotsky's death that made it possible to develop the theory of bureaucratic state capitalism. It was the transformation of Eastern Europe into Stalin's satellites that led me to question whether Trotsky's description of Russia as a degenerated workers' state was adequate.

What prevented Trotsky from renouncing the theory that Russia was a workers' state?

One tends to see the future in the trappings of the past. For many years the fight against exploitation took the form of a fight against the owners of private property—the bourgeoisie. Therefore, when Lenin, Trotsky and the rest of the Bolshevik leaders said that if the workers' state of Russia remained isolated it was doomed, they envisaged that doom in a definite form—the restoration of private property. State property was seen as the fruit of the struggle of working people. From here it was only one step to Trotsky's conclusion that if state ownership existed in Russia it was thanks to the bureaucracy's fear of the working class, and that this meant the bureaucracy was not free to carry through a counter-revolution that restored capitalism, private ownership and the right of inheritance.

Past experience was Trotsky's main impediment in grasping the fact that a triumphant reaction did not inevitably mean a return to the original point of departure. Capitalism could result from a decline, in spiral form, in which elements of the pre-revolutionary and of the revolutionary pasts were combined. The old capitalist class content could then emerge cloaked in new 'socialist' clothing, thus serving as further confirmation of the law of combined development—a law that Trotsky himself did so much to develop.

In summing up, it may be said that, while Trotsky contributed incomparably more than any other Marxist to an understanding of the Stalinist regime, his analysis suffered from one serious limitation—a conservative attachment to formalism. This is by its nature contradictory to Marxism which subordinates form to content.

Towards the denouement of the Stalinist regime

The assumption that the Stalinist regime was inherently superior to capitalism, that it was more progressive, was summed up in Trotsky's assertion that in Russia the productive forces developed very dynamically as against the 'stagnation and decline in almost the whole capitalist world'.[53] Of course, for a Marxist the relative progress of one regime over another is above all expressed in its ability to develop the productive forces further.

In line with Trotsky's statement that the Soviet regime demonstrated the ability to speedily develop the productive forces far beyond what capitalism was able to achieve, Ernest Mandel wrote in 1956:

> The Soviet Union maintains a more or less even rhythm of economic growth, plan after plan, decade after decade, without the progress of the past weighing on the possibilities of the future...all the laws of development of the capitalist economy which provoke a slowdown in the speed of economic growth are eliminated.[54]

In the same year, 1956, Isaac Deutscher prophesied that ten years later the standard of living in the USSR would surpass that of Western Europe!

A state capitalist analysis of the Russian regime pointed in an exactly opposite direction: the bureaucracy was, and would become, more and more a brake on the development of the productive forces. The 1948 document 'The Class Nature of Stalinist Russia' had pointed out that, while the bureaucracy's role was to industrialise Russia by raising the productivity of labour, in the process it entered into sharp contradictions:

> The historical task of the bureaucracy is to raise the productivity

of labour. In doing this the bureaucracy enters into deep contradictions. In order to raise the productivity of labour above
a certain point the standard of living of the masses must rise,
as workers who are undernourished, badly housed and uned-
ucated are not capable of modern production.[55]

Up to a point the bureaucracy could raise the productivity
of labour by coercion, but this cannot go on indefinitely. Failure to raise living standards might have already been leading
to a decline in the rate of productivity growth, and to 'jerky developments of production'.[56]

In 1964 a 100 page update to a new edition of the book on
Russian state capitalism under the title *Russia: A Marxist
Analysis* pointed out that the Soviet economy inherited from
Stalin was more and more paralysed by elements of crisis, and
became more and more of a dead weight on the development
of production:

> Stalin's method of approach to each new failure or difficulty was
> to increase pressure and terrorism. But this rigid method
> became not only more and more inhumane but also more and
> more inefficient. Each new crack of the whip increased the
> stubborn, even if mute, resistance of the people...rigid Stalin-
> ist oppression became a brake on all modern industrial
> progress.[57]

The book made a detailed examination of how the Stalinist regime became a block on all branches of the economy.
On the crisis in agriculture it said:

> The legacy Stalin left in the countryside is an agriculture bogged
> down in a slough of stagnation that has lasted over a quarter
> of a century. Grain output in 1949-53 was only 12.8 percent
> larger than in 1910-14 while at the same time the population
> increased by some 30 percent. Productivity of labour in Soviet
> agriculture has not reached even a fifth of that in the United
> States.
>
> The stagnation became a threat to the regime for a number
> of reasons. First, after the hidden unemployment in the coun-
> tryside was largely eliminated, it became impossible to siphon
> off labour to industry on the former scale without raising labour
> productivity in agriculture. Secondly, it also became impossi-
> ble beyond a certain point to siphon off capital resources from

agriculture to aid the growth of industry. Stalin's method of 'primitive capital accumulation' from being an accelerator, became a brake, which slowed down the entire economy.[58]

What about industry? Although it had expanded massively over some three and a half decades, the rate of growth was declining. Productivity, which had grown more rapidly than in the West in the 1930s, was now stuck at a considerably lower level than in Russia's major rival, the United States:

> At the end of 1957 the number of industrial workers in the USSR was 12 percent larger than in the United States... Nevertheless, even according to Soviet estimates, the product turned out annually by industry in the USSR in 1956 was half that in the United States.[59]

Because of the crisis in agriculture, the lower level of productivity in industry could no longer be compensated for by a massive growth in the number of industrial workers. So the Russian bureaucracy had to pay increasing attention to the proliferation of waste and lower quality output within the Russian economy.

Several of the sources of waste were spelt out in the book: the compartmentalism that led enterprises to produce goods internally that could be produced more cheaply elsewhere;[60] the hoarding of supplies by managers and workers;[61] the tendency of managers to resist technological innovation;[62] the stress on quantity at the expense of quality;[63] the neglect of maintenance;[64] the proliferation of 'paper work and muddle';[65] the failure to establish the efficient and rational price mechanism which managers required if they were to measure the relative efficiency of different factories.[66] The conclusion was:

> If by the term 'planned economy' we understand an economy in which all component elements are adjusted and regulated into a single rhythm, in which frictions are at a minimum, and, above all, in which foresight prevails in the making of economic decisions, then the Russian economy is anything but planned. Instead of a real plan, strict methods of government dictation are evolved for filling the gaps made in the economy by the decisions and activities of this very government. Therefore, instead of speaking about a Soviet planned economy, it would be much more exact to speak of a bureaucratically directed economy.[67]

Of course many other people offered descriptions of inefficiencies in Russian industry. What characterised the above account was the way the waste and inefficiency were seen as the product of the state capitalist nature of the system. The basic causes of anarchy and wastage in Russian industry were held to be capitalist accumulation in an isolated economy—high targets of output together with low supplies.

Like the two arms of a nutcracker these pressed upon the managers, encouraging them to cheat, cover up production potentialities, inflate equipment and supply needs, play safe by hoarding resources, and in general act conservatively. This led to wastage, and hence further lack of supplies and increasing pressures from above on the manager, who once more had to cheat, and so on in a vicious circle.

High targets and low supplies also led to increasing departmentalism, looking after one's own sector at the expense of the economy in general—again a vicious circle. The same problem led managers to prioritise. But this priority system and 'campaign' methods lacked a clear quantitative gauge and led to wastage and distortions. To combat these features a multiplicity of control systems arose which were in themselves wasteful and in their lack of systematisation and harmony made for even further wastage. Hence the need for more control, for paper pyramids and a plethora of bureaucrats. Again a vicious circle. The vicious circle resulting from the conflict between over-ambitious plan targets and low supply basis applied, *mutatis mutandis*, to the effect of the poor price mechanism. This in turn encouraged still more departmentalism, priority campaigns and a plethora of controls.

Behind all of these problems lay capitalist imperatives—the world competition for power and the tremendous military expenditure required to survive it.

Low productivity was caused not only by mismanagement from above, but also by workers' resistance from below. It was impossible to judge exactly the extent to which this low productivity was a result of mismanagement and blunders at the top or workers' resistance. The two aspects naturally could not be divorced. Capitalism in general, and its bureaucratic state capitalist species in particular, was concerned with cutting costs and raising efficiency rather than with satisfying human needs. Its rationality was basically irrational, as it alienated the worker, turning him into a 'thing', a manipulated object, instead of a subject who moulds his life according to his own desires. That was why workers sabotaged production.[68]

The chapter on Russian workers concluded with these words:

> A central worry for the Russian leaders today is how to develop the productivity of the worker. Never has the attitude of the workers to their work meant more to society. By the effort to convert the worker into a cog of the bureaucrats' productive machine, they kill in him what they most need, productivity and creative ability. Rationalised and accentuated exploitation creates a terrible impediment to a rise in the productivity of labour.
>
> The more skilled and integrated the working class, the more will it not only resist alienation and exploitation, but also show an increasing contempt for its exploiters and oppressors. The workers have lost respect for the bureaucracy as technical administrators. No ruling class can continue for long to maintain itself in face of popular contempt.[69]

Bureaucratic state capitalism was sinking into a deeper and deeper general crisis. As Marx explained, when a social system becomes a brake on the development of the productive forces, the epoch of the revolution commences.

Post-mortem on the Stalinist regime

A post-mortem reveals the deep sickness that affected a person when alive. Thus the moment of death of a social order can be its moment of truth. When in the autumn and winter of 1989 the East European regimes installed by Stalin's army began to collapse, followed by the collapse of 'Communism' in the USSR itself, a clear judgement on the nature of the Stalinist regime was thereby facilitated.

The perception of the Stalinist regime as socialist, or even a 'degenerated workers' state'—that is, a transitional stage between capitalism and socialism—assumed that it was more progressive than capitalism. For a Marxist this signified first of all that it was able to develop the productive forces more efficiently than capitalism. We need only to remember Trotsky's words:

Socialism has demonstrated its right to victory, not on the pages of *Das Kapital*, but in an industrial arena comprising a sixth part of the earth's surface—not in the language of dialectics, but in the language of steel, cement and electricity.[70]

Indeed it was the language of industrial development that explained events in Eastern Europe and the USSR. But what had happened was not victory but a slowing down of economic growth in the late 1970s and early 1980s leading to stagnation and a growing gap between these countries and the advanced West.

In the USSR the annual rate of growth of gross national product was as follows: the first Five Year Plan (though an exaggerated claim), 19.2 percent; 1950-59, 5.8 percent; 1970-78, 3.7 percent; in 1980-82 it was down to 1.5 percent; during its final three or four years there was a negative rate of growth.[71]

If the productivity of labour had been more dynamic in Eastern Europe and USSR than in the West, one could not understand why the rulers of these countries eventually became enamoured of the market. Then again, the reunification of Germany should have seen the flourishing of East German industry in comparison with that of West Germany. In fact the economy of East Germany has collapsed since unification. The number of workers employed in East Germany in 1989 was ten million, while now it is only six million. Productivity of labour in East Germany is only 29 percent of the Western level.[72] Thus the East German productivity level, though the highest in Eastern Europe, was still low compared with West Germany and other advanced economies that it now had to compete with.

If the USSR had been a workers' state, however degenerated, it is obvious that if capitalism assaulted it the workers would have come to the defence of their state. Trotsky always considered it axiomatic that the workers of the Soviet Union would come to its aid if attacked by capitalism, however corrupt and depraved the bureaucracy dominating it. A favourite analogy of Trotsky's was between the Soviet bureaucracy and the trade union bureaucracy. There are different kinds of trade union—militant, reformist, revolutionary, reactionary, Catholic—but all are defence organisations of the workers' share in the national cake. Trotsky argued that, however reactionary the bureaucrats dominating the trade unions, workers would always be 'supporting their progressive steps and...defending them against the bourgeoisie.'

When it came to the crunch in 1989 the workers in Eastern Europe did not defend 'their' state. If the Stalinist states were workers' states one cannot explain why their only defenders were the Securitate in Romania, the Stasi in East Germany, and so on, or why the Soviet working class supported Yeltsin, the outspoken representative of the market.

If the regime in Eastern Europe and the USSR was post-capitalist and in 1989 there was a restoration of capitalism, how was the restoration achieved with such astonishing ease? The events do not square with Trotsky's assertion that the transition from one social order to another must be accompanied by civil war. Trotsky wrote:

> The Marxist thesis relating to the catastrophic character of the transfer of power from the hands of one class into the hands of another applies not only to revolutionary periods, when history sweeps madly ahead, but also to the period of counter-revolution, when society rolls backwards. He who asserts that the Soviet government has been gradually changed from proletarian to bourgeois, is only, so to speak, running backwards the film of reformism.[73]

The 1989 revolutions in Eastern Europe were remarkable for the absence of large scale social conflict and violence. Except for Romania there was no armed conflict. As a matter of fact there were fewer violent clashes in East Germany, Czechoslovakia and Hungary than took place between the police and striking miners in Thatcher's Britain.

The transition from one social order to another is necessarily accompanied by the replacing of one state apparatus by another. The state machines were hardly touched in 1989. In Russia the Soviet army, the KGB and the state bureaucracy are still in place. In Poland the military helped to promote the change. General Jaruzelski, the architect of the 1981 coup, and the interior minister and chief administrator of martial law, General Kizcak, played a crucial role in negotiating the round table agreement with Solidarity, and the formation of Mazowiechi's coalition government.

If a counter-revolution had taken place, if a restoration of capitalism had taken place, there should have been a wholesale replacement of one ruling class with another. Instead we witnessed the continuity of the same personnel at the top of society; the members of the nomenklatura who ran the economy, society and state under 'socialism' now do the same under the 'market'. Mike Haynes, in his very good article 'Class and Crisis: the Transition in Eastern Europe', writes:

> What it [the state] has succeeded in doing has been to partly shift the institutional base of its power out of a 'state pocket' and into a 'private pocket'. In the process there has been some upward mobility within the ruling class and the occasional new entrant. There has also been a change in the balance of power within the ruling class between its sections. But, contrary to those who claim that what was at stake was the substitution of the socialist mode of production...by a capitalist society, there is no evidence that a fundamental change has taken place in the nature of the ruling class. What is striking is how little change has actually occurred. To sack a general and promote a colonel hardly constitutes a social revolution any more than selling off a state enterprise to its managers does or renationalising it with a similar group of people in control. Rather it suggests that what is at stake is an internal transformation within a mode of production, in this instance a shift in the form of capitalism from one of strong state capitalism to more mixed state and market forms.[74]

Chris Harman aptly described the development as 'moving sideways'—a shift from one form of capitalism to another, from bureaucratic state capitalism to market capitalism.

Finally, if the USSR and East European countries had had a post-capitalist economic and social order, how was it possible that a capitalist market economy could be grafted onto it? One can graft a lemon onto an orange tree, or vice versa, because both belong to the same family—the citrus; one cannot graft a potato onto an orange tree. Mike Haynes describes the successful grafting of market capitalism onto the Stalinist economy:

> It is precisely because both sides of the transition show the same structural features that individual opportunism on the scale we have analysed has been possible. We are not merely

looking at class societies, but class societies rooted in a common mode of production where what has been changing has been the form rather than the essence. Unless this is understood it becomes impossible to understand how, beneath the turnover at the top, the same people, the same families, the same social networks are still toasting their good fortune in the 1990s as they had toasted in the 1980s. It is true that as they chatter and socialise they might on occasion spare a thought for some of their absent friends but they will not lose sight of the greater whole— that they are still on top despite the transitions. Beneath them is the same working class, still carrying the burden of their wealth, privilege and their incompetence as it has done in the past.[75]

The people who were the real victims of the old order are now also the real victims of the new.[76]

If the expansion of the state capitalist regime into Eastern Europe put the theory of the degenerated workers' state into question, the collapse of the Stalinist regime answered that question unequivocally. In both cases the theory of bureaucratic state capitalism demonstrated itself as a viable alternative.

Trotsky's work in analysing the degeneration of the Russian Revolution and the rise of Stalinism as a product of the pressure of international capitalism on a workers' state in a backward country was a pioneering effort. Trotsky played a crucial role in opposing Stalin's doctrine of 'socialism in one country'. His thoroughly Marxist, historical materialist approach to the Stalinist regime was crucial to the development of the theory of bureaucratic state capitalism. It is necessary to defend the spirit of Trotskyism while rejecting some of his words.

My criticism of Trotsky's position was intended as a return to classical Marxism. Historical development—especially after Trotsky's death—demonstrated that the 'degenerated workers' state' position was not compatible with the classical Marxist tradition which identified socialism as the self emancipation of the working class. To preserve the spirit of Trotsky's writing on the Stalinist regime, the letter of his writing had to be sacrificed. The end of fake socialism in the USSR and Eastern Europe is opening up opportunities for the rediscovery of the real revolutionary ideas of Lenin and Trotsky, the true legacy of the October Revolution. Despite the so called 'fall of Communism', the concluding words of my *State Capitalism in Russia* are as true as when they were written:

> The final chapter can be written only by the masses, self mobilised, conscious of socialist aims and the methods of their achievement, and led by a revolutionary Marxist party.

> The state capitalist definition of the Stalinist regime followed Trotsky's theory of permanent revolution in taking the capitalist world system as its basic frame of reference:

> ...when Russia is viewed within the international economy the basic features of capitalism can be discerned: 'Anarchy in the social division of labour and despotism in that of the workshop are mutual conditions of each other...'[77]

The theory was able to explain the subjection of the working class in Russia to the dynamic of capitalist accumulation by setting the Stalinist regime in its global context, the international state system dominated by military competition.

Chapter 3

The permanent arms economy

After the Second World War market capitalism boomed in the West. This ran directly counter to Trotsky's prediction, which was still being parroted by Mandel and others. The effort to resolve this contradiction led to the formulation of the theory of the permanent arms economy.

To understand how it came about it will be useful to make a short diversion of an autobiographical nature. The fact that in Palestine I had independently built a small Trotskyist group—some 30 members—from scratch was a valuable preparation for wrestling with the great difficulties the international Trotskyist movement faced at the end of the Second World War. I was like the little child in Hans Christian Andersen's story of the emperor's new clothes. After years of isolation and torment under Nazism and Stalinism, the Trotskyists suffered from the psychological need to believe in miracles. The real situation was too painful to face. Had my political development been as part of the British Trotskyist organisation, which in 1946 had some 400 members, I would probably have been under pressure to conform. It was not in itself enough to escape dogmatism that I had read Marx, Engels, Lenin, Trotsky and Luxemburg. Mandel and Pablo were no less knowledgeable in Marxist literature than myself. Being an isolated Palestinian in Britain was, in retrospect, a political advantage.

Coming to Britain in 1946, and viewing the conditions here from the perspective of a colonial country, I was struck by the fact that:

...the standard of living for workers was high. When I first visited a worker's house—just an ordinary house—I asked his job and he was an engineer. My English wasn't very good so I thought he meant an engineer with a degree. But he was a semi-skilled engineering worker. It was a complete shock. Children were better off than in the 30s. The only time I saw children without shoes in Europe was in Dublin. Children didn't get rickets any more. This helped me to realise that the final crisis wasn't just around the corner.[78]

Some people in the Trotskyist movement had little difficulty in dealing with the mismatch between the long boom and the prediction. Gerry Healy continued to live in a fantasy world of imminent capitalist catastrophe. Mandel always lagged behind events and used woolly formulations regarding the working mechanism of capitalism. Instead of clarification he exuded confusion.[79] The first polemical article I wrote on the subject challenged Mandel and appeared in 1947. It was a critique of his attempt to deny the existence of a post-war economic recovery but as yet it did not go beyond rejecting a mechanical concept of Marxian economics.[80]

An effective understanding of the general issue did not have to grapple only with the problems raised by the failure of Trotsky's prediction. It also had to deal with the prophets of an eternal capitalist boom, who argued that the system would thrive so long as Keynesian economic policies were followed.

Full employment was a fact after the Second World War, but to assume that it was a result of Keynesian policies is like believing that the cock crowing causes the sunrise. From 1928 onwards John Maynard Keynes argued that the primary responsibility of government was to use fiscal and monetary policies to ensure that there was enough effective demand in the economy to maintain full employment. In 1936 Keynes developed his ideas further in his book *General Theory of Employment, Interest and Money*. But at no time was his advice followed in practice by the governments of the period. Neither the Conservative, Labour nor National governments accepted Keynes's argument.

Things did change with the looming of war. The capitalists, who were very reluctant to spend money on public works in peacetime, as Keynes recommended, were now very generous in splashing out money to the military. Thus, for instance, the United States capitalists who had been very angry with Roosevelt for incurring an annual budget deficit of over $2billion to over $4 billion (1934, $3.6 billion; 1935, $3.0 billion; 1936, $4.3 billion; 1937, $2.7 billion) did not mind a deficit of $59 billion in 1941-42. It is unlikely that Hitler read Keynes's *General Theory* but he did achieve full employment by mobilising millions into the army and the arms industry. It was the arms race, not a Cambridge economist, that made the difference.

However, when, for the first time in two decades, full employment was finally reached, the idea that this could be maintained by state demand management became very widespread. For leading politicians of all parties in the post-war generation the doctrine put forward by Keynes appeared to have been fully vindicated.

Even a number of ex-Marxists declared themselves to be adherents of Keynes. Among them was John Strachey. In 1932-35 Strachey wrote three books, *The Coming Struggle for Power*, *The Menace of Fascism* and *The Nature of the Capitalist Crisis*, in which he claimed to be an orthodox Marxist (even though he was in fact much influenced by Stalinism). In 1940 Strachey published a new book, *A Programme for Progress*. This argued that, while in the long run socialism was the only remedy for the breakdown of capitalism, in the short run what was needed was an interim programme for reforming capitalism similar to that of Roosevelt's New Deal. His programme included six main points: the extension of public enterprise, low interest rates on loan capital, increased social services, monetary allowances to individuals, and redistributive taxation. There would also be a state controlled banking system and strict public control over the balance of payments.[81] This programme was so minimalist that the right winger Anthony Crosland could say, 'It was incomparably more modest than the programme the Labour Party adopted in 1937'.[82] John Strachey continued to pay homage to some of Marx's analyses and to describe society as 'capitalist'. But he now concluded that unemployment and crises were a thing of the past. Mass democracy and the techniques of government economic intervention discovered by Keynes, he said, meant that capitalism now was planned.

Crosland too waxed lyrical about a capitalism reformed by Keynesian methods. His book *The Future of Socialism,* published in 1956, argued that the anarchy of capitalism was withering away, and so also were class conflicts. The system was becoming more and more rational and democratic. Capitalism itself would peacefully dissolve. All the talk about production being dedicated to making profits rather than meeting human need was, according to Crosland, sheer nonsense. 'Private industry is at last becoming humanised'.[83] A 'peaceful revolution' had begun in which class conflict would be unthinkable: 'One cannot imagine today a deliberate offensive alliance between government and employers against the unions,' wrote Crosland.[84] 'We stand, in Britain, on the threshold of mass abundance'.[85]

Now that Keynesianism guaranteed uninhibited growth, said Crosland, the state could look forward to high tax revenues which could finance social reforms and social welfare plans. Socialists should divert their attention away from economic issues. To what?

> ...we shall turn our attention increasingly to other and, in the long run, more important spheres—of personal freedom, happiness, and cultural endeavour; the cultivation of leisure, beauty, grace, gaiety, excitement...more open air cafes, brighter and gayer streets at night, later closing hours for public houses, more local repertory theatres, better and more hospitable hoteliers and restaurateurs...more murals and pictures in public places, better designs for furniture and pottery and women's clothes, statues in the centre of new housing estates, better designed street lamps and telephone kiosks, and so on ad infinitum.[86]

If Mandel and Healy were refuted by the immediate conditions of the post-war boom, the Keynesians and other apologists for capitalism have been confounded in the longer term by the increasingly deep and intractable crises that have swept Western capitalism since the 1970s.

The theory of the permanent arms economy avoided the traps of both positions. It grew out of the development of the theory of state capitalism. Understanding Russia became the key to unlocking an understanding of the post-war boom in

Western capitalism. Why was this so?

The theory of state capitalism identified military competition between Russia and the Western capitalist countries as the chief mechanism enforcing the dynamic of capital accumulation in Russia. Armaments production in Russia also explains why it did not suffer from the cycle of boom and slump. The converse was also true—on the other side of the Iron Curtain arms spending remained at a high level even though the Second World War had ended.

The 1948 document 'The Class Nature of Stalinist Russia' has a chapter called 'Production and Consumption of Means of Destruction'. Arms production has peculiar properties. It neither provides new means of production (Department I, to use Marx's terminology in *Capital*), nor contributes to the consumption of the working class (Department IIa). The output of the arms industry, therefore, does not feed back into further production. It is a form of unproductive consumption, analogous to the consumption of luxuries by the capitalists themselves (Department IIb or III).[87]

Armaments production is 'the collective consumption of the capitalist class' which ensures that that class through military expansion will 'get new capital, new possibilities of accumulation'. The ability to acquire new possibilities of accumulation distinguishes the 'production and consumption of means of destruction' from other consumption of the capitalist class.

'The Class Nature of Stalinist Russia' pointed out that the stabilising properties of arms production explained why Russian state capitalism did not experience the classical cycle of boom and slump characteristic of market economies.[88] The above analysis was a bridge to the theory of the permanent arms economy which stresses the role of military expenditure in the expansion of the economy of the market capitalist countries.

In May 1957 the argument became more specific in the article entitled 'Perspectives for the Permanent War Economy' that moved from the effect of military expenditure on the dynamics of Stalinist Russia to its effect on the capitalism of the West and Japan.[89] The impact of arms spending was not seen as an accident. The economic level of society, the level its productive forces have reached, is the decisive factor in the organisation of its armies. As Marx said, 'Our theory that the organisation of labour is conditioned by the means of production is, it seems, nowhere as brilliantly corroborated as in the "human slaughter industry".'

In the early period of capitalism the backwardness of the economy made it impossible to feed and arm large armies. Compared with the mass armies mobilised during the First and Second World Wars, the armies of early rising capitalism were very small. Even during the Napoleonic Wars, France, ruler of practically the whole of Europe, did not at any time have more than half a million troops. The British armed forces at the time were less than a tenth of those of France. Frederick the Great declared of the wars of the 18th century, 'The peaceful citizen should not even notice that the country is at war'.[90] Even during the wars of the 19th century, the Napoleonic Wars, the Opium Wars, the Crimean War, etc, the life of the belligerent nations was on the whole hardly affected.

1914—the turning point

All this changed with the First World War. Then France, whose population was only some ten million more people than during the Napoleonic times (40 million against 30), mobilised as many as five million soldiers. The other belligerent countries showed similar increases. Together with the tremendous increase in the size of the armies there came a massive increase in spending on military technology. Together these brought a change in the role of the military sector in the overall national economy.

With a significant proportion of the population mobilised and a major portion of the economy harnessed to the service of war, not only the soldiers engaged in battle, but also millions of industrial workers, agricultural workers and peasants, etc—in fact, the whole civilian population—felt the impact.

Before the First World War, although the imperialist powers were to some extent prepared for battles, the economy was hardly geared to armament production at all. It was only after the various wars had actually started that the ruling class made decisions to cope with the situation it was now squarely faced with—guns or butter.

Up to 1914, therefore, it was possible to analyse the development of capitalism without paying much attention to wars or preparations for them, as they played a minor role in economic development. Immediately after the First World War the military sector of the economy again dwindled: the large armies were to a major extent demobilised and armaments production was drastically cut.

However, in the wake of the great slump of the 30s and Hitler's rise to power, a powerful peacetime military sector appeared for the first time in history. Between 1939 and 1944 the production of munitions multiplied in Germany five times, in Japan ten times, in Britain 25 times, and in the United States 50 times.[91]

The war economy

	Germany (billion marks)		Britain (£ million)		United States ($ million)	
	1939	1943	1938	1943	1939-1940	1944-1945
GE**	60.0*	100.0*	1.0	5.8	16.0	95.3
NI	88.0*	125.0*	5.2	9.5	88.6*	186.6*
GE/NI	68%	80%	19.2%	61.1%	18%	51%

GE = government expenditure, NI = national income
* approximate figures
** mainly arms spending

Whereas after the First World War there was a period of about a decade and a half in which no advanced country had a relatively large war sector, after the Second World War there was no such break. Soon after its end the armaments race was once again on.

Arms, boom and slump

Previously, for more than a century, capitalism went through a rhythmical cycle of prosperity and slump. Slumps occurred more or less regularly every ten years. But since the advent of a permanent war economy the cycle had somehow been broken. To understand how this came about, how a military sector of some 10 percent or less of the national economy could prevent general slump, we should first shortly sum up the causes of slump under classical capitalism.

The basic cause of capitalist crises of overproduction is the relatively low purchasing power of the masses compared with the production capacity of industry. As Marx said:

> The ultimate reason for all real crises always remains the poverty and restricted consumption of the masses as opposed to the drive of capitalist production to develop the productive forces as though only the absolute consuming power of society constituted their limit.[92]

In the final analysis, the cause of the capitalist crisis is that a greater and greater part of the income of society falls into the hands of the capitalist class and a greater and greater part of this is directed not towards buying means of consumption, but instead means of production—that is, it is directed towards the accumulation of capital. The relative increase in the part of the national income directed to accumulation compared with the part directed towards consumption must lead to overproduction, a situation where the increasing quantity of goods that are made cannot be sold because consumers do not have the means to buy them.

This is a cumulative process. An increase in accumulation is accompanied by rationalisation and technological innovation, resulting in an increased rate of exploitation. The greater the rate of exploitation, the greater is the fund from which accumulation is drawn as compared with the wages of the workers and the revenue of the capitalist. Accumulation breeds accumulation.

Effect of arms budget

The gigantic military expenditures after the war affected the tendency to crisis. Now the armaments economy had a very great influence on the level of popular purchasing power, the level of real capital accumulation, and the amount of goods seeking a market.

Let us assume that there are a million people seeking employment in a certain country and, further, that 10 percent of them are employed by the government in producing arms—some 100,000 people. Their purchasing power would bring about the employment of more people elsewhere. The numerical relation between the size of the first group and the second was called the 'multiplier' by Keynes. For brevity this term can usefully be borrowed. If the multiplier is two, the employment of 100,000 workers by the state will increase general employment by 200,000. If the multiplier is three, the increase will be 300,000, and so on. Hence there is no doubt that the cumulative effect of an arms budget of 10 percent of the national income can be quite out of proportion to its size in increasing the purchasing power of the masses.

Again, when 10 percent of the national income goes to arms, the capital resources seeking investment in peacetime production are drastically cut: in our example, from 20 percent of the national income to 10 percent. The increased purchasing power of the people, together with the new state demand for arms, army clothing, barracks, etc, gives greater openings for sale and staves off crises of overproduction.

In addition, a war economy naturally has a big effect on the rate of increase of the supply of non-military goods seeking civilian purchasers. Full employment not only increases the overall number of people earning a wage, it causes a tightness in the labour market which enables workers to win higher wages. Paradoxically, this does not deny the possibility of increasing profits: capital is working more fully than otherwise; there is much less idle capacity or capital working at a loss. Its turnover is greater. Thus, for instance, in the years 1937-42 total wages in United States industry rose by 70 percent, profits by 400 percent!

With the stupendous productive forces available to society, the increase in the armaments burden did not necessarily lead to a cut in civilian consumption, but the contrary. This was shown most clearly in the richest capitalist country in the world, the United States, during the Second World War. Although in 1943 the United States spent the huge sum of $83.7 billion on the war, civilian consumption did not fall but was actually higher than before the war, rising from $61.7 billion in 1939 to $70.8 billion in 1943 (expressed in 1939 prices), an increase of 14.7 percent.

The permanent arms economy theory showed why Trotsky's prediction had not been validated. But it did more. It demonstrated that in the long run an economic prosperity rising on top of the cone of a nuclear bomb could not be stable and safe. Even when world capitalism was prosperous, as a result of the military expenditure, not all countries carried the same burden of high military budgets. Those which spent little benefited in inverse proportion to arms expenditure. The 1948 document on Russia argued that capitalism generally was experiencing only a temporary stabilisation. It stated:

> ...the powers may compete so fiercely on the world market that each, in order to strengthen its position, would start to cut arms expenditure. We are at present witnessing Britain being pushed to cut her 'defence budget' through competition with Germany, and deterioration of her international balance of payments. Up to now no country has been able to match the United States, force her to abandon the arms race and start competing on 'who cuts the arms budget quickest'. She can afford the greatest military budget in the world and the greatest absolute investment in industry.[93]

The uneven burden of the arms race would lead to destabilisation although the document predicted, wrongly as it turned out, that Russia might be the winner:

> ...with the huge strides of Russian industry, it is possible that in another ten or 20 years, she may, even if she does not reach the absolute level of United States industry, at least challenge the United States on the world market in certain branches—those of heavy industry. Then the United States may...cut the defence budget in order to circumvent defeat on the world market.[94]

Nevertheless the basic argument was correct:

> The war economy may thus less and less serve as a cure for overproduction, a stabiliser of capitalist prosperity. When the war economy becomes expendable, the knell of the capitalist boom will surely toll.[95]

In fact it was not Russia which forced the United States to cut its military budget, but primarily West Germany and Japan, the two countries forbidden to maintain large armies because they lost the war. Nevertheless, 'The Class Nature of Stalinist Russia' was right to foresee that the temporary stabilisation of market capitalism through arms expenditure would only be temporary. Indeed, by diverting surplus value from productive investment it tended to prevent slumps at the price of a long term tendency towards stagnation. Those economies with a relatively high level of military expenditure would find themselves at a competitive disadvantage and would therefore be forced to increase the share of investment going to civilian industries. This allowed the tendencies towards a classical business cycle to reassert themselves.[96]

The growing rivalry between the United States on the one hand and Japan and West Germany on the other, sharpened by the uneven distribution of the arms burden, did lead to destabilisation of the economy and a return to global recessions. The prognosis that after a number of years the world economy would slow down has come true: world output that rose annually by 5.4 percent in the years 1950-63, and 6 percent in the years 1963-73, declined to 2.6 percent in the years 1973-90, and 1.4 percent in the years 1990-96.[97]

The United States spent a far greater proportion of its national income on armaments than Japan or West Germany. Japan never spent more than 1 percent of its national income on defence. As a result Japan managed to accumulate more capital and to invest more in industry to retool its factories. The outcome was that the Japanese car industry shot ahead in leaps and bounds. The Japanese shipbuilding industry replaced the British industry as first in the world, and in electronics Japan surpassed Germany which had hitherto held first place, etc, etc.

The Vietnam War exacerbated the lag of United States industry relative to that of Germany and Japan. The result was that in 1973 the weakness of the dollar revealed itself in an explosion in the price of oil—denominated in dollars. The long boom was at an end.

The theory of the permanent arms economy took it for granted that the irrationality of capitalism did not lessen with the ageing of the system. Capitalism, which in Marx's words was covered throughout history in blood and mud, did not become more benevolent in old age. As a matter of fact the permanent arms economy is the most extreme expression of the bestiality and barbarism of the system.[98]

Chapter 4

Deflected permanent revolution

One further issue which post-war Trotskyists had difficulty in understanding concerned developments in the Third World. The theory of permanent revolution as developed by Trotsky in Russia predicted the weakening of imperialism and social change in Third World countries. This was to be driven by the working class struggling to complete the tasks of the bourgeois revolution and at the same time carrying on through to the struggle for socialism. The issue of whether Trotsky's theory of permanent revolution adequately explained the significant developments in the Third World was posed most sharply in Mao's China and Castro's Cuba. Did the theory apply? To this question neither a 'yes' nor a 'no' would do. There was a lot in common between what happened in these two countries and Trotsky's theory, but in some ways there was also a radical divergence. Hence the need arose to formulate a theory that could encompass both aspects. This was the theory of deflected permanent revolution.

Mao's rise to power

Despite its 'Communist' label, the industrial working class played no role whatsoever in the victory of Mao's Chinese Communists over the Nationalist Kuomintang in 1949. Even the social composition of the Chinese Communist Party itself was completely non-working class. Mao's rise in the party ranks coincided with a time when it ceased to be a working class party. Towards the end of 1926 at least 66 percent of the membership were workers, another 22 percent intellectuals and only 5 percent peasants.[99] By November 1928 the percentage of workers had fallen by more than four fifths to just 10 percent. An official report admitted that the party 'did not have a single healthy party nucleus among the industrial workers'.[100] A year later workers comprised only 3 percent of the membership and this dropped to virtually nothing by the end of 1930.[101] From then on and until Mao's final victory the party had virtually no industrial workers.

For a number of years the party was confined to insurgent peasant movements deep in the provinces of central China, where it established a Chinese Soviet Republic; later, after a military defeat in the central provinces in 1934, it moved to northern Shensi in the north west. In both these areas there was no industrial working class to speak of. A Comintern organ was not exaggerating when it wrote, 'The Border Region is socially and economically one of the most backward regions of China'.[102] Chu Teh repeated, 'The regions under the direction of the Communists are the most backward economically in the whole country'.[103] Not one real town came under the control of the Communists until a couple of years before the establishment of the Chinese People's Republic.

So unimportant were workers in Communist Party strategy during the period of Mao's rise to power that the party did not find it necessary to convene a National Congress of Trade Unions in the 19 years following the one held in 1929. It did not bother to seek workers' support, as witnessed in its declaration that it did not intend to maintain any party organisation in Kuomintang-controlled areas during the crucial years 1937-45.[104] When, in December 1937, the Kuomintang government decreed the death penalty for workers who went on strike or even agitated for a strike while its war against the Japanese was in progress, a Communist Party spokesman told an interviewer that the party was 'fully satisfied' with that government's conduct of the war.[105] Even after the outbreak of civil war between the Communist Party and the Kuomintang, hardly any Communist Party organisations existed in the

Kuomintang areas, which included all the industrial centres in the country.

Mao's conquest of the towns revealed more than anything else the Communist Party's complete divorce from the industrial working class. Communist leaders did their best to prevent any workers' uprisings in the towns on the eve of their being taken. Before the fall of Tientsin and Peking, for example, General Lin Piao, commander of the People's Liberation Army, issued a proclamation calling on people:

> ...to maintain order and continue in their present occupations. Kuomintang Yuan officials or police personnel of provincial, city, country or other level of government institutions; district, town, village, or Pao Chia (Kuomintang security) personnel...are enjoined to remain at their posts.[106]

At the time of the crossing of the Yangtze River, before the great cities of central and south China (Shanghai, Hankow, Canton) fell to them, Mao and Chu Teh issued a proclamation in identical terms:

> ...workers and employees in all trades will continue to work...officials of the Kuomintang central, provincial, municipal or county governments of various levels, or delegates of the 'National Assembly', members of the Legislative and Control Yuans or People's Political Council members, police personnel and heads of Pao Chia organisations...are to stay at their posts.[107]

The working class obliged and remained inert. A report from Nanking on 22 April 1949, two days before the People's Liberation Army occupied it, described the situation in this way:

> Nanking's population is showing no signs of excitement. Curious crowds were seen this morning to gather at the river wall to watch the gun duel on the opposite side of the river. Business is going on as usual. Some shops are closed, but it is due to lack of business... Movie houses are still showing to packed houses.

A month later a *New York Times* correspondent wrote from Shanghai, 'The Red troops began putting up posters in Chinese instructing the populace to be calm and assuring them they had nothing to fear'.[108] In Canton 'after their entry the Communists made contact with the police station and instructed the officers and men to remain at their posts to keep order'.[109]

Trotsky's argument that the tasks of the bourgeois revolution such as liberation from imperialist domination could only be achieved by workers could not explain what happened in China.

Castro's revolution

Another example of developments that did not fit Trotsky's scenario occurred in Cuba. Here neither the working class nor even the peasantry played a serious role. Middle class intellectuals filled the whole arena of struggle in Fidel Castro's rise to power. C Wright Mills's book, *Listen Yankee*, which is a more or less authentic monologue spoken by the Cuban leaders, deals first of all with what the revolution was not:

> ...the revolution itself was not a fight...between wage workers and capitalists... Our revolution is not a revolution made by labour unions or wage workers in the city or by labour parties, or by anything like that...the wage workers in the city were not conscious in any revolutionary way; their unions were merely like your North American unions: out for more money and better conditions. That was all that really moved them. And some were even more corrupt than some of yours.[110]

After discussions with Cuban leaders, Paul Baran, an uncritical supporter of Castro, wrote:

> It would seem that the employed segment of the industrial working class remained, on the whole, passive throughout the revolutionary period. Forming the 'aristocratic' layer of the Cuban proletariat, these workers partook of the profits of monopolistic business—foreign and domestic—were well paid by Latin American standards, and enjoyed a standard of living considerably higher than that of the masses of the Cuban people. The fairly strong trade union movement was dominated by 'business unionism', United States style, and was thoroughly permeated by racketeering and gangsterism.[111]

The indifference of the industrial proletariat accounted for the complete failure of Castro's call for a general strike on 9 April 1958, some 16 months after the beginning of the uprising and eight months before the fall of the Cuban dictator, Batista. The workers were apathetic; and the Communists sabotaged it. It was some time later that they jumped on Castro's bandwagon.[112]

Not only was the working class uninvolved in the rise of Castro, the same applied to the peasantry. As late as April 1958 the total number of armed men under Castro numbered only about 180 and at the time of Batista's fall had only grown to 803.[113] The cadres of Castro's bands were intellectuals. Those small numbers of peasants who did participate were not agricultural wage earners. Che Guevara described the peasants who joined Castro in the Sierra Maestra:

> The soldiers that made up our first guerrilla army of country people came from the part of this social class which shows its love for the possession of land most aggressively, which expresses most perfectly the spirit catalogued as petty bourgeois.[114]

The Castro movement was middle class. The 82 men under Castro who invaded Cuba from Mexico in December 1956 and the 12 who survived to fight in the Sierra Maestra all came from this class. 'The heaviest losses were suffered by the largely middle class urban resistance movement, which created the political and psychological acids that ate into Batista's fighting force'.[115]

Characteristically for the Cuban movement, Che Guevara implied that the industrial working class would be irrelevant to all future socialist revolutions:

> The *campesinos*, with an army made up of their own kind fighting for their own great objectives, primarily for a just distribution of land, will come from the country to take the cities... This army, created in the countryside, where subjective conditions ripen for the seizure of power, proceeds to conquer the cities from the outside...[116]

Elsewhere in the Third World the working class never played more than a subsidiary role in post-war social transformations, and even when present it was not acting as an independent force striving for revolutionary socialism as had been the case in Russia during 1917. Therefore the processes of overcoming internally backward socio-economic relations and achieving national liberation from imperialism were spearheaded by a variety of forces mostly drawn from the intelligentsia, or the state, playing the part ascribed to the working class in Trotsky's permanent revolution theory. Although the political results in Africa, Asia and Latin America varied, state capitalism was, to a greater or lesser extent, the prevailing result.

What had gone wrong with Trotsky's theory of permanent revolution?

The basic elements of Trotsky's theory can be summed up in six points:

(1) A bourgeoisie which arrives late on the capitalist scene is fundamentally different from its ancestors of a century or two earlier. It is incapable of providing a consistent, democratic, revolutionary solution to the problems posed by feudalism and imperialist oppression. It is incapable of carrying out the thoroughgoing destruction of feudalism, the achievement of real national independence and political democracy. It has ceased to be revolutionary, whether in the advanced or backward countries. It is an absolutely conservative force.

(2) The decisive revolutionary role falls to the proletariat, even though it may be very young and small in number.

(3) The peasantry, incapable of independent action, will follow the towns, and in view of the first two points, must follow the leadership of the industrial proletariat.

(4) A consistent solution of the agrarian question, of the national question, a break up of the social and imperial fetters preventing speedy economic advance, will necessitate moving beyond the bounds of bourgeois private property: 'The democratic revolution grows over immediately into the socialist, and thereby becomes a permanent revolution'.[117]

(5) The completion of the socialist revolution 'within national limits is unthinkable... Thus, the socialist revolution becomes a permanent revolution in a newer and broader sense of the

word; it attains completion only in the final victory of the new society on our entire planet'.[118] It is a reactionary, narrow dream to try and achieve 'socialism in one country'.

(6) As a result, revolution in backward countries would lead to convulsions in the advanced countries.

While the conservative, cowardly nature of a late developing bourgeoisie (Trotsky's first point) is an absolute law, the revolutionary character of the young working class (second point) is neither absolute nor inevitable. If the working class is not, in fact, revolutionary, then points (3) to (5) will not be realised.

Once the unswervingly revolutionary nature of the working class, the central pillar of Trotsky's theory, becomes suspect, the whole structure falls to pieces. His third point is not realised, as the peasantry cannot follow a non-revolutionary working class, and all the other elements follow suit. But this does not mean that nothing at all happens. A concatenation of national and international circumstances brings the productive forces into conflict with the fetters of feudalism and imperialism. Peasant rebellions take on a deeper, broader sweep than ever before. In them is rooted also national rebellion for higher living standards and against the economic ruin brought by imperialism. The result was a type of transformation which included elements of permanent revolution but also deviated from it in radical ways. This we called deflected permanent revolution, a theory that was first presented in broad terms in 1963.[119]

If the two main classes of modern capitalist society, the capitalists and the workers, were not playing a key role—one because it had become a conservative force, the other because it was diverted from its goal by Stalinism or reformism—how could such a major process occur? The drive of the productive forces plus the rebelliousness of the peasantry would not by themselves have been sufficient to break the yoke of landlordism and imperialism. Four other factors helped:

(1) The weakening of world imperialism as a result of increasing contradictions between the two superpower blocs whereby each felt paralysed by the existence of the H-bomb. This partially limited their ability to intervene in the Third World for fear of igniting a war with each other.

(2) The growing importance of the state in backward countries. It is one of the tricks of history that when a historical task faces society, and the class that traditionally carries it out is absent, some other group of people, quite often organised as a state power, implements it. Under such conditions state power plays a very important role. It reflects not only, or even mainly, the national economic base on which it rises, but the supra-national imperatives of the world economy.

(3) The impact of Stalinism and reformism diverting the strength of the workers' movements in a different direction to socialist revolution. Very often Communist parties, or similar movements with influence among the working class, put their efforts into collaborating with and bolstering local forces representing other class interests.

(4) The growing importance of the intelligentsia as the leader and unifier of the nation, and above all as manipulator of the masses. This last point will need special elaboration.

The leading role of the intelligentsia in a revolutionary movement is in direct proportion to the general backwardness—economic, social and cultural—of the masses from whose midst it arises. It is characteristic that the Russian Populist movement, which more than any other emphasised the need to revolutionise the most backward elements of society, the peasants, was also the group to put the greatest premium on the intelligentsia, masters of 'critical thinking'.

The revolutionary intelligentsia proved itself a much more cohesive factor in the emergent post-war nations than in Tsarist Russia. With native bourgeois private property too weak to transform the situation, and the burden of imperialism felt as intolerable, state capitalism seemed the answer. Through the weakening of imperialism, the growing importance of state planning, the example of Russia, and the organised, disciplined work of the Communist parties, it gave the intelligentsia a cohesive programme. As the only non-specialised section of society (because it was not locked into a particular class role within the relations of production) the intelligentsia was both the source of a 'professional revolutionary elite' and simultaneously appeared to represent the interests of the 'nation' as against conflicting sectional and class interests. In addition, it was the section of society most imbued with the national culture, the peasants and workers having neither the leisure nor education for that.

The intelligentsia were also sensitive to their countries' technical lag. Participating in the scientific and technical world of the 20th century, they were stifled by the backwardness of their own nation. This feeling was accentuated by the 'intellectual unemployment' endemic in these countries. Given the general economic backwardness, the only hope for most students is a government job, but there are not nearly enough of these to go round.[120]

The spiritual life of the intellectuals was also in crisis. In a crumbling order where the traditional pattern was disintegrating, they felt insecure, rootless, lacking in firm values. Dissolving cultures gave rise to a powerful urge for a new integration that had to be total and dynamic if it was to fill the social and spiritual vacuum. The intelligentsia embraced nationalism with a religious fervour.

Before their country gained political freedom, the intellectuals found themselves under dual pressure—privileged beyond the majority of their people, yet subordinated to the foreign rulers. This explains the hesitations and vacillations so characteristic of their role in the national movements. Their advantages created a feeling of guilt, of 'debt' towards the 'dark' masses, and at the same time a feeling of being divorced from and superior to them. The intelligentsia are anxious to belong without being assimilated, without ceasing to remain apart and above. They were in search of a dynamic movement which would unify the nation, opening up broad new vistas for it, but which at the same time would give the intelligentsia itself power.

They were great believers in efficiency, including efficiency in social engineering. They hoped for reform from above and would dearly have loved to hand the new world over to a grateful people, rather than see the liberating struggle of a self conscious and freely associated people result in a new world for themselves. They cared a lot for measures to drag their nation out of stagnation, but very little for democracy. They embodied the drive for industrialisation, for capital accumulation, for national resurgence. Their power was in direct relation to the feebleness of other classes, and their political nullity.

All this made totalitarian state capitalism a very attractive goal for intellectuals. And indeed, they were the main banner bearers of Communism in the emergent nations. 'Communism has found greatest acceptance in Latin America among students and the middle class,' wrote a Latin American specialist.[121] In India, at the Congress of the Communist Party in Amritsar (March/April 1958), 'approximately 67 percent of the delegates were from classes other than the proletariat and peasantry (middle class, landowning class and 'small traders'); 72 percent had some college education'.[122] In 1943 it was found that 16 percent of all party members were full time functionaries.[123]

Deflected permanent revolution

In the Third World Trotsky's theory suggested that the driving forces of social development would lead to permanent revolution and workers struggling for socialism. But in the absence of the revolutionary subject, proletarian activity and leadership, the result could be a different leadership and a different goal—state capitalism. Using what was of universal validity in Trotsky's theory (the conservative character of the bourgeoisie) and what was contingent (upon the subjective activity of the proletariat), one came to a variant that, for lack of a better name, was called the 'deflected, state capitalist, permanent revolution'. However, the central theme of Trotsky's theory remains as valid as ever: the proletariat must continue its revolutionary struggle until it is triumphant the world over. Short of this target it cannot achieve freedom.

Chapter 5

The heritage

The present essay began by juxtaposing Trotsky's prognoses regarding the world situation after the Second World War and the actual state of affairs. This was followed by describing how the great majority of Trotskyists closed their eyes to reality while remaining true to Trotsky's words, thus deviating completely from his spirit. Trotsky could rightly have said, 'I have sowed dragons' teeth but harvested fleas.' Why did this happen? Why did Mandel, Pablo and other leading Trotskyists, who were very serious and not stupid, behave as they did and live in a fantasy world? The reason was that for years of dark reaction—of Nazism and Stalinism—the Trotskyists found themselves very isolated with hardly a foothold in the working class. In the desert for such a long time, thirsty for water, they succumbed to hallucinations, seeing a mirage of green trees and a world of water.

Trying to be true to the essence of the teachings of Marx, Lenin, Luxemburg and Trotsky, and come to terms with the real situation in the world after the Second World War, the International Socialist tendency made the effort to develop three pieces of theory: the definition of Stalinist Russia as state capitalist which explained its long stability and eventual demise; the long boom of Western capitalism rooted in the permanent arms economy but containing the seeds of future crises; and an explanation of Mao's and Castro's victories in terms of deflected permanent revolution.

Were there practical links in the real world which meant that there was a link between these three theories?

Indeed there were. The survival and strength of the Stalinist regime in Russia was the key to the other two developments.

First of all, Stalinist influence played a crucial role in preventing the deep social and political tensions at the end of the Second World War from turning into proletarian revolutions. The social tensions on the continent of Europe were much sharper and deeper now than at the end of the First World War which detonated revolutions in Russia, Germany, Austria, Hungary and near revolutionary situations in a host of other countries. If such open revolution did not occur in 1945 it was because of the Communist parties. Using their radical aura the Stalinist leaders were able to play a crucial role in damming up the rising tide of revolution and in defending capitalism.

The examples of France, Italy and Germany illustrate the potential that was lost. In August 1944 it was the Resistance, led by the Communist Party, that liberated Paris from the Nazi troops: complete control fell into its hands. Compare the Communists with rival political groups. Gabriel Kolko's *The Politics of War* explains that 'the Resistance groups that were Gaullist in ideology were always in a small minority. In many key parts of France they hardly existed at all'.[124] The Socialist Party was equally lacking in popular support:

> The Socialists had been the party par excellence of the Third Republic and their compulsive devotion to remaining in politics, even after Vichy, eventually resulted in the party's expelling two thirds of its National Assembly members for collaboration and compromise. After 1941 the Socialists literally disappeared as a party, and only gradually began reconstituting their ranks in 1944.[125]

This left the field free for the Communist Party: 'The Communist dominated Resistance organisation, the *Francs-Tireurs et Partisans*...was the largest'.[126] Ian Birchall describes the situation in France as follows:

> The liberation of France from Nazi occupation in the second half of 1944 left the country in a state of turmoil. Initially central government had little control over the situation. In various municipalities liberation committees were set up; in Marseilles the local authorities began a programme of regional public ownership without even consulting Paris. People's courts were set up and some 11,000 collaborators shot.

The liberation committees were mostly controlled by the French Communist Party and the government was powerless to intervene, the minister of the interior appealing in vain for them to stop acting autonomously. Only the intervention of Maurice Thorez, French Communist Party leader, could restrain them. He insisted:

> Local liberation committees must not substitute themselves for municipal and departmental administration, just as the National Council of the Resistance has not substituted itself for the government.[127]

It was Maurice Thorez who, on returning from Moscow to France, issued the call, 'One police. One army. One state.' And so the Resistance was disarmed. Kolko writes:

> Thorez disciplined the older, militant leadership around André Marty and Charles Tillon, whom he ultimately expelled; he banned strikes and demanded more labour from the workers, and endorsed the dissolution of the [Resistance organisations]. Every social objective he subordinated to the objective of winning the war; 'the task of Liberation Committees is not to administer,' he told the party Central Committee in January 1945, 'but to help those who administer. They must, above all, mobilise, train, and organise the masses so that they attain the maximum war effort and support the Provisional Government in the application of the programme laid down by the Resistance.' In brief, at the critical point in the history of French capitalism, the party of the left refused to act against it. 'The unity of the nation', Thorez never tired of reiterating, was a 'categorical imperative'... The party helped to disarm the Resistance, revive a moribund economy, and create sufficient stability to give the old order a crucial breathing spell—and later took much pride in the accomplishment.[128]

If anything, in Italy the wave of revolution rose even higher. Pierre Broué writes, 'In Italy it was the workers' agitation—and no one will be surprised to learn that it began in the Fiat plant—which finally shook the ground under the fascists' regime, and dug the grave of Benito Mussolini'.[129]

The strike in the massive Fiat plant turned into a general strike that brought the regime down the next day. A year later:

> In March 1944...a new and even more impressive protest

spread through occupied Italy. This time the slogans of the strikers were more political, demanding immediate peace and an end to war production for Germany. The numbers involved exceeded the most optimistic forecasts; 300,000 workers came out in the province of Milan. In the city itself tram workers struck on 1 March, and were only forced back on the 4th and 5th by a terror campaign against them. The strike spread beyond the industrial triangle to the textile factories of the Veneto and the central Italian cities of Bologna and Florence. Women and lower paid workers were in the forefront of the agitation. At one time or another in the first week of March hundreds of thousands of workers downed tools.[130]

The industrial, political and armed struggle of the Italian working class rolled on relentlessly which meant that by 1945 working class districts in Turin were effectively no-go areas for fascists and the Germans.[131] Eventually:

By 1 May the whole of northern Italy was free. The popular and insurrectionary character of the liberation, which left an indelible impression in the memories of those who had participated, was welcomed in most quarters. In others it caused acute anxiety. There was a terrible settling of scores, with perhaps as many as 12,000-15,000 people being shot in the immediate aftermath of the liberation. As for the northern industrialists, they had hoped for a painless transition of power from the fascists to the Anglo-American authorities. Instead they found their factories occupied, the workers armed, and a period of up to ten days between the insurrection and the arrival of the Allies. Some of the more heavily compromised of them did not dare to wait and fled to Switzerland. Over the next few months the fear of imminent social revolution remained very strong in capitalist circles.[132]

That this revolution did not materialise was above all due to the control exercised by the Italian Communist Party. Broué writes:

The Italian Communist Party—that section of the Communist International directly under the control of Moscow—made approaches to the notables, the renegade fascists, the marshals and the princes of the church, to propose a compromise to them that was to save all of them from the pressure from the streets in exchange for a government ministry, and hence legal recognition for the Italian Agency in Moscow.[133]

Like Thorez in France, a key role was played by the Italian Communist leader, Togliatti, who returned from a long stay in Moscow. Ginsburg writes:

> On his arrival in Salerno, Togliatti outlined to his comrades, amidst a certain astonishment and some opposition, the strategy which he intended the party to pursue in the near future. The Communists, he said, were to put into abeyance their oft-expressed hostility to the monarchy. Instead they were to persuade all the anti-fascist forces to join the royal government, which now controlled all of Italy south of Salerno. Joining the government, Togliatti argued, was the first step towards realising the overriding objective of the period—national unity in the face of the Nazis and fascists. The main aim of the Communists had to be the liberation of Italy, not a socialist revolution.
>
> Togliatti insisted that the unity of the war years should, if possible, be continued into the period of reconstruction. This grand coalition was to embrace not only the Socialists, but also the Christian Democrats (DC). In a speech in Rome in July 1944 he characterised the DC as a party which had in its ranks 'a mass of workers, peasants, intellectuals and young people, who basically share our aspirations because like us they want a democratic and progressive Italy'.[134]

> In April 1944 Togliatti argued for the parties of the Committee of National Liberation to swear allegiance to the king and join the government of Marshal Badoglio. He had been commander in chief under Mussolini and leader of the Italian troops who invaded Abyssinia in 1935. Togliatti even became one of Badoglio's ministers![135]

In Germany revolutionary struggle was even more difficult than in France and Italy, yet even here there was an unfulfilled potential for revolution. It is true that Nazi repression made resistance to the Third Reich extremely difficult, but this was only one side of the equation. The potential for fighting back was also systematically undermined from within the anti-Nazi camp. Disastrous political leadership by the reformist Social Democratic Party (SPD) and above all the Communist Party

(KPD) under Stalinist control left German workers bitter and confused as Hitler was allowed to come to power without a finger being lifted against him.

The signing of the Hitler-Stalin pact in 1939 broke the spirits of the German Communists who formed the only mass resistance to Nazism. A sign of this was that Gestapo seizures of underground leaflets dropped from 15,922 in 1939 to just 1,277 in 1940.

Even when the war was under way Allied tactics seemed calculated to discourage revolt against the Third Reich and to produce instead a sullen loyalty. In the East, Stalin claimed to be fighting the 'Great Patriotic War' and the target shifted from being the Nazi regime to all Germans. The anti-German, practically racist propaganda of Russia undermined the development of a resistance movement to the Nazis. Again and again Ilya Ehrenburg, writing in the Russian press, repeated the sentence, 'The only good German is the dead German.' I remember a short article by him in which he described how a German soldier, facing a Russian one, put his hands up and said, 'I'm the son of a blacksmith'—what better formulation of working class identification! What was the reaction of the Russian soldier? Ehrenburg writes, 'The Russian soldier said, "You are a German and responsible for the crimes of the Germans," and then dug his bayonet into the chest of the German soldier.'

German soldiers ended the First World War by revolution against the Kaiser, but in the conditions of the Second World War no such revolt emerged, for as one soldier put it, 'God forbid we lose the war. If revenge comes upon us, we'll have a rough time.'

But still the seeds of revolution were there. At the end of the Second World War the heavy lid of repression was lifted off German workers and they were given a real chance to express themselves. What was revealed was amazing. A gigantic movement of anti-fascist committees, or 'Antifas', swept across Germany as each new area was liberated from Nazism. There were well over 500 of these committees, which were overwhelmingly working class in composition. For a brief time, between the overthrow of the Nazi regime and the reimposition of 'order' by the occupying Allied forces (Russia in the East, Britain and the United States in the West), workers were free in a double sense.

Not only had Nazi tyranny disappeared, but Gestapo rule had temporarily disrupted the deadening influence of both the reformist Social Democratic leaders and the Stalinist Communist Party.

The Antifas grew explosively. In Leipzig (East Germany) there were 38 local committees claiming 4,500 activists and 150,000 adherents. Despite the distractions caused by the devastation of war (the population had fallen from 700,000 to 500,000, for example), up to 100,000 people turned out on their 1945 May Day demonstration. In Bremen (West Germany), a city where 55 percent of the homes were uninhabitable and one third of the population had fled, there were 14 local groups, claiming 4,265 members. A fortnight later the figure was 6,495. Many Antifas were organised in the workplaces. In the central Ruhr soon after the liberation an assembly of workplace representatives included 360 delegates from 56 pits and many other enterprises.

The Antifas were determined to rip out Nazism. Strikes were launched demanding a purge of Nazi activists. In Bremen and elsewhere the buildings of the Nazi union, the German Labour Front, were taken over. Returning concentration camp inmates were housed in the spare rooms of Nazi activists and the most notorious of the latter were handed over to the authorities. Stuttgart went further and set up its own 'revolutionary tribunals'.

There was an awareness that only by the workers doing the job themselves could Nazism really be banished for good. The Prince Regent mine in Bochum called for a political general strike and issued the slogan, 'Long live the Red Army', not in reference to the Soviet forces but to the insurrectionary force of the 1918-23 German Revolution. The view was advanced that 'in the future state there will be no more employers as previously. We must all arrange it and work as if the enterprise is ours!' In some places workers took over their factories and management fled. Antifas set up their own factory militias and replaced police chiefs and mayors with their own nominees. The situation in Stuttgart and Hanover was described as one of 'dual power', the Antifas having set up their own police forces, taken over a raft of powerful local positions and begun to run vital services like food provisioning.

The eyewitness report of a United States official is worth citing at length:

> In widely dispersed areas under a number of different names and apparently without any connection one with the other, anti-Nazi unity front movements emerged soon after the collapse of the Nazi government... Although they have no contact with each other, these groups show a remarkable similarity in the way they are constituted and their programme. The initiative for their creation appears in each case to come from people who were active during the Nazi period and in some form or another were in contact with each other... Denunciation of Nazis, efforts to prevent an illegal Nazi underground movement, de-Nazification of civil authorities and private industry, improvement of housing and food supply provision—these are the central questions which preoccupy the newly created organisations... The conclusion is therefore justified, that these communities represent the spontaneous coming together of anti-Nazi resistance forces, which, as long as the terror regime remained, were powerless.

The report went on to contrast the activities of the left, which emphasised uprooting all traces of Nazism as the precondition of a new start and the right which 'concentrated on the attempt to preserve out of the ruins of the Hitler regime anything that might still be usable'.

Alas, the Antifas could only exist in each locality for a few weeks because they were opposed not only by the occupation forces (including the Russian army) but by Stalinists in the workers' movement. As soon as the occupying forces gained a firm grip of the local area they were banned. This applied as much to the Russian-controlled Eastern sector as to the West. The Antifas were dissolved with the connivance of both workers' parties. After the agreement at Yalta the Stalinist KPD accepted that the Western allies had full rights to control their sphere of influence and would tolerate no independent action in the East either. In the West the reformist SPD had no interest in promoting revolution. So the period in question was brief—just a few weeks in each locality during the spring of 1945. Nevertheless, they showed the potential for workers' power which was blocked, in large part by Stalinism from above and below.[136]

Chapter 6

Conclusion

If the Stalinist regime had not survived the war, as Trotsky prophesied, of course the Stalinist parties of France and Italy would not have had the massive power to preserve capitalist order in these countries. Similarly, the German working class would not have been paralysed after the fall of Hitler.

The survival of state capitalism led to the survival of Western capitalism, for it was in the interests of both to avoid revolution. But this is a system of hostile brothers and the former wartime allies were soon involved in a massively costly arms race—the Cold War. This was the basis for the permanent arms economy that operated in the West.

The linkage between the existence of the Stalinist regime in Russia and deflected permanent revolution in China and Cuba is more obvious. It was the existence of a strong Russia that inspired the Maoist armies to go on fighting against Japanese imperialism for many years, and also against Chiang Kai-shek's Kuomintang. It was the example of forceful and speedy industrialisation of backward Russia under Stalin that inspired the Stalinist parties and emerging governments throughout the Third World and was a model for them to follow. The Stalinist policy of allying with local pro-capitalist forces meant that imperialism was not overthrown by workers' revolution. Imperialism was frequently able to disengage itself politically from the colonies without having to give up its economic stranglehold. Where state capitalist policies were followed alliances with the Russian bloc might be forged, but the situation of workers was still one of exploitation and subordination to capitalist rule.

Therefore, once Trotsky's prognosis about the fate of the

Stalinist regime in Russia was not realised, the rest of his prognoses—about developments in the advanced capitalist countries as well as in the backward countries—also failed to materialise.

The troika—state capitalism, the permanent arms economy, and deflected permanent revolution—make a unity, a totality, grasping the changes in the situation of humanity after the Second World War. This is an affirmation of Trotskyism in general, while partially its negation. Marxism as a living theory must continue as it is, and change at the same time. However, the troika was not conceived as a unity and did not come into being in a flash. It was the result of several long explorations into economic, social and political developments in three portions of the globe: Russia and Eastern Europe, the advanced industrialised capitalist countries, and the Third World. The paths of research criss-crossed each other again and again. But it was only at the end of the process that the interrelationships between the different spheres of research became clear. Only at the top of the mountain can one see the relationship between the different footpaths designed to reach the summit and from this vantage point the analysis turns into a synthesis, the Marxist dialectic emerging victorious.

Grasping the real changes in the structure of economy, society and politics in the world, with the massive unevennesses tearing it apart, makes it possible to grasp the real, actual, concrete possibilities for revolutionaries to place themselves in the process of change.

Today the Stalinist regime in Russia and Eastern Europe is no more. World capitalism is not propelled forward by the permanent arms economy. The state capitalist road to economic growth in the Third World has been abandoned as closer global economic integration narrows the room for manoeuvre of local ruling classes or groups aspiring to play that role. Across the world—West, East, and in the developing countries—millions of workers have been sacked; tens of millions of unemployed live side by side with an increasing number of millionaires and multi-millionaires.

The troika—the definition of Russia as state capitalist, the permanent arms economy as an explanation for the post-war economic boom in the advanced capitalist countries, and deflected permanent revolution as an explanation for the success of Maoism in the Third World—might look irrelevant to today's Marxists. But it is not so.

First of all, ideas survive, quite often for a long time after the material conditions that brought them to life have disappeared; a ripple in the water caused by the dropping of a stone continues even after the stone stops moving.

Thus illusions about the Stalinist regime still survive among supporters and bourgeois opponents alike. The idea that state ownership of industry and economic planning, even without workers' democracy, is equal to socialism, is still alive.

It was the full or near full employment that followed the outbreak of the Second World War that strengthened the attraction of Keynesianism. The theory of the permanent arms economy has been the only serious Marxist alternative to Keynesianism to explain the situation at the time. Keynesianism is still alive and kicking and is today being presented as the economic alternative to free market economics.

The ideas of Maoism are still quite attractive to people, especially in the Third World. The image of Che Guevara still has a great resonance in Latin America. The idea that only the working class organising itself in a struggle for socialism led by revolutionary Marxists can achieve revolution is not widely held in national liberation movements.

There is another reason why the three theories we deal with need to be studied. It is to do with the nature and continuity of the Marxist tradition. As Trotsky put it, the revolutionary party is the memory of the working class. Prior to Trotsky's death this memory, the actual continuity of the movement, was represented by a mass of individuals. This can be shown in concrete terms.

The First International was made up of relatively large organisations, and although there was a break of some two decades between the end of the First and establishment of the Second International, many thousands who were members of the First joined the Second. The Third International (the Communist International, or Comintern) came into being as a result of large splits within the Second International. The Italian Socialist Party, at its conference in Bologna in September 1919, voted to join the Communist International, adding

300,000 members. In Germany the Independent Social Democratic Party, which split in 1917 from the Social Democratic Party, also decided to join the Communist International, adding another 300,000 members. In 1920 the French Socialist Party joined, adding 140,000 members. In June 1919 the Bulgarian Socialists voted to affiliate, bringing 35,478 members. The Yugoslav Socialist Party, also a mass party, joined. The Czechoslovak Social Democratic Party split in December 1920, the Communist Left taking over half the membership and establishing a Communist Party of 350,000 members. A separate split in the Social Democratic Party of the German speaking minority added further forces, and after their unification the party claimed 400,000 members. The Norwegian Labour Party joined the Comintern in spring 1919. In Sweden the majority of the Socialist Party, after a split, joined the Comintern, adding another 17,000.[137]

Sadly, there was hardly any continuity in terms of individual revolutionaries between the Communist International of Lenin and Trotsky in the early 1920s and the Trotskyist movement in the 1930s and after the Second World War. Crushed between the massive influence of Stalin and fear of Hitler, Trotskyist organisation always consisted of tiny groups on the margins of the mass movements. Thus the number of Trotskyists in Berlin on the eve of Hitler's victory was 50![138] Despite the Spanish Revolution of 1936, in September 1938, according to the report of the Founding Conference of the Fourth International, the membership of the Spanish section was between ten and 30![139]

The First, Second and Third Internationals came into life in periods of working class advance; the Trotskyist organisations were born during a dire period of working class history—the victory of Nazism and Stalinism. Without understanding why for two generations Trotskyism was isolated and powerless and therefore Trotskyists were prone to losing their way, one must come to completely pessimistic conclusions about the future. Understanding the past makes it clear that Trotskyism, as a link in the continuity of Marxism, is coming into its own.

Now Stalinism, the great bulwark preventing the advance of revolutionary Marxism, of Trotskyism, has gone. Capitalism in the advanced countries is no longer expanding and so the words of the 1938 Transitional Programme that 'there can be no discussion of systematic social reforms and the raising of the masses' living standards' fits reality again.[140] The classic theory of permanent revolution, as argued by Trotsky, is back on the agenda, as shown by the Indonesian Revolution of 1998.

The troika explains why for a time, a long time, the existing system—capitalism—persevered, even if it adopted a number of guises. At the same time it always pointed to the processes undermining this stability: for some time these processes were at the molecular level and barely visible on the surface. But eventually quantity changes into quality and the system as a whole is racked by crises and instability. Then, as Marx put it, humanity 'will leap from its seat and exultantly exclaim, "Well burrowed, old mole!"'[141]

Notes

1   K Marx, *The Civil War in France* (Moscow, 1977).
2   L Trotsky, *Writings 1934-35* (New York, 1974), pp181-182.
3   L Trotsky, *Writings 1933-34* (New York, 1975), p316.
4   L Trotsky, *Writings 1935-36* (New York, 1977), p260.
5   L Trotsky, *In Defence of Marxism* (London, 1971), pp16-17.
6   W Reisner (ed), *Documents of the Fourth International* (New York, 1973), p183.
7   M Kidron, *Western Capitalism Since the War* (London, 1970), p11.
8   T Cliff and D Gluckstein, *The Labour Party: A Marxist History* (London, 1988), p227.
9   Ibid, p253.
10   L Trotsky, *Writings 1938-39* (New York, 1974), p78.
11   L Trotsky, *Writings 1937-38* (New York, 1976), p27.
12   L Trotsky, *Writings 1938-39*, op cit, p87.
13   See T Cliff, *Trotsky: The Darker the Night the Brighter the Star* (London, 1993), p198.
14   Ibid, p383.
15   Ibid, p109.
16   This statement was made in November 1945. See J P Cannon, *The Struggle for Socialism in the 'American Century'* (New York, 1977), p200.
17   *Fourth International*, April 1946.
18   Ibid.
19   *Fourth International*, June 1946.
20   E Germain (Mandel), 'The Soviet Union After the War', *Fourth International*, September 1946.
21   *Fourth International*, June 1948.
22   *Fourth International*, August 1948.
23   Quoted in T Cliff, *Neither Washington Nor Moscow* (London, 1982), pp84-85.
24   See 'On the Class Nature of Yugoslavia', published in the October 1949 issue of *International Information Bulletin*.
25   Internal Bulletin of the LSSP, Ceylon, April 1954, p7.
26   Ibid, p15.
27   Robert J Alexander, *International Trotskyism* (Durham and London, 1991), p664.
28   Ibid, p334.

29   Ibid, pp663-664.
30   *Fourth International*, June 1946.
31   Ibid.
32   Ibid.
33   Ibid.
34   Ibid.
35   E Germain (Mandel), 'The First Phase of the European Revolution', in *Fourth International*, August 1946.
36   E Germain (Mandel), 'Problems of the European Revolution', in *Fourth International*, September 1946.
37   E Germain (Mandel), 'From the ABC to Current Reading: Boom, Revival or Crisis?' A refutation of Mandel's attempt to deny the evidence of economic recovery was carried out by T Cliff in an article called 'All that Glitters is not Gold' reprinted in T Cliff, *Neither Washington Nor Moscow*, op cit, pp24-39.
38   Ibid, p61.
39   K Marx and F Engels, *The Communist Manifesto* (Peking, 1990), p59.
40   F Engels, *Anti-Dühring* (Moscow, 1975), p336.
41   R Luxemburg, *Gesammelte Werke*, vol 3 (Berlin, nd), pp63-64.
42   For an elaboration of this argument see T Cliff, *Neither Washington Nor Moscow*, op cit, pp65-66.
43   Ibid, pp66-67.
44   L Trotsky, *Problems of the Development of the USSR: A Draft of the Theses of the International Left Opposition on the Russian Question* (New York, 1931), p36.
45   *New International*, April 1943.
46   Ibid.
47   See, for example, L Trotsky, *The Revolution Betrayed* (New York, 1974), p289.
48   K Marx, *The Poverty of Philosophy* (London, nd), pp129-130.
49   Ibid, p161.
50   K Marx, *A Contribution to the Critique of Political Economy* (Chicago, 1918), pp285-286.
51   T Cliff, *State Capitalism in Russia* (London, 1988), pp221-222.
52   Ibid, pp165-166.
53   L Trotsky, *The Revolution Betrayed*, op cit, p6.
54   E Mandel, in *Quatrième Internationale*, no 14, 1956.
55   T Cliff, 'The Class Nature of Stalinist Russia' (London, 1948), pp134-135.
56   Ibid.
57   T Cliff, *Russia: A Marxist Analysis* (London, 1964), pp197-198.
58   Ibid, p198.
59   Ibid, p240.
60   Ibid, p287.
61   Ibid, p256.
62   Ibid, p256.
63   Ibid, p254.
64   Ibid, p257.
65   Ibid, pp248-249.
66   Ibid, pp250-254.
67   Ibid, pp273-274.
68   Ibid, p283.

69 Ibid, pp309-310.

70 L Trotsky, *The Revolution Betrayed*, op cit, p8.

71 The national income of the Comecon bloc rose annually as follows: 1951-55, 10.8 percent; 1956-60, 8.5 percent; 1961-65, 6.0 percent; 1966-70, 7.4 percent; 1971-75, 6.4 percent; 1976-80, 4.1 percent; 1981-85, 3 percent; 1986-88, 3 percent. *Statisticheskii ezhegodnik stran—Chlenov soveta ekonomicheskoi vzaimopomoshchi* (Moscow, 1989), p18.

72 *Financial Times*, 12 May 1992.

73 L Trotsky, *Writings 1933-34*, op cit, pp102-103.

74 M Haynes, 'Class and Crisis: the Transition in Eastern Europe', *International Socialism* 54, Spring 1992, pp46-47.

75 Ibid, p90.

76 Ibid, p69.

77 T Cliff, *State Capitalism in Russia*, op cit, pp221-222.

78 T Cliff, 'Fifty Five Years a Revolutionary', *Socialist Review* 100, May 1987, pp14-19, reprinted in L German and R Hoveman (eds), *A Socialist Review* (London, 1998), pp15-28.

79 See, for example, E Mandel, *Late Capitalism* (London, 1975).

80 T Cliff, 'All that Glitters is not Gold', op cit, pp24-37.

81 J Strachey, *A Programme for Progress* (London, 1940), pp210-211.

82 A Crosland, *The Future of Socialism* (London, 1956).

83 Ibid, p37.

84 Ibid, pp32-33.

85 Ibid, p23.

86 Ibid, pp520-522.

87 See T Cliff, 'The Class Nature of Stalinist Russia', op cit, pp121-122.

88 Ibid, pp121-125.

89 T Cliff, 'Perspectives for the Permanent War Economy', *Socialist Review*, March 1957, reprinted in T Cliff, *Neither Washington Nor Moscow*, op cit, pp101-107.

90 Quoted ibid, p101.

91 F Sternberg, *Capitalism and Socialism on Trial* (London, 1951), p438.

92 K Marx, *Capital*, vol III, ch 30: 'Money Capital and Real Capital' (Moscow, 1959), p484.

93 T Cliff, 'The Class Nature of Stalinist Russia', op cit, pp121-125; T Cliff, *Neither Washington Nor Moscow*, op cit, pp106-107.

94 Ibid, p107.

95 Ibid, p107.

96 Ibid, p107.

97 *Financial Times*, 4 September 1998.

98 Further big steps in the development of the theory of the permanent arms economy were taken by Mike Kidron and Chris Harman. See M Kidron, *Western Capitalism Since the War* (London, 1970) and *A Permanent Arms Economy* (London, 1989), and C Harman, *Explaining the Crisis* (London, 1984).

99 R C North, *Kuomintang and Chinese Communist Elites* (Stanford, 1962), p32.

100 H R Isaacs, *The Tragedy of the Chinese Revolution* (London, 1938), p333.

101 Ibid, p394.

102 *World News and Views*, 22 April 1939.

103 S Gelder, *The Chinese Communists* (London, 1946), p167.

104 See *Communist Manifesto* published in Chungking, 23 November 1938, re-

ported in the *New York Times*, 24 November 1938.

105 H R Isaacs, op cit, p456.

106 New China News Agency, 11 January 1949.

107 Ibid, 3 May 1949.

108 *New York Times*, 25 May 1949.

109 *South China Morning Post*, 17 October 1949.

110 C Wright Mills, *Listen Yankee* (New York, 1960), p47.

111 P A Baran, *Reflections on the Cuban Revolution* (New York, 1961), p17.

112 The Communist Party of Cuba, the People's Socialist Party, had a lot to live down. It supported Batista's rule between 1939 and 1946. It participated in Batista's first ministry with two ministers. In 1944 the Communist paper *Hoy* addressed Batista as the 'idol of a people, the great man of our national policy, the man who incarnates the sacred deals of a new Cuba'. Castro was declared a petty bourgeois adventurer. As stated above, the Communists did not cooperate in the April 1958 strike. As late as 28 June 1958 they were timidly advocating 'clean democratic elections' to get rid of Batista. See P A Baran, op cit.

113 Speech by Castro of 1 December 1961, 'El Mundo La Habana', 22 December 1961.

114 Che Guevara, 'Cuba: Exceptional Case?', *Monthly Review* (New York), July-August 1961, p59.

115 T Draper, 'Castro's Cuba. A Revolution Betrayed?' *Encounter* (London), March 1961.

116 Che Guevara, op cit, p63.

117 L Trotsky, *The Permanent Revolution* (New York, 1978), p278.

118 Ibid, p279.

119 T Cliff, 'Deflected Permanent Revolution', first published in *International Socialism* 12 (first series), spring 1963.

120 Thus, for instance, a survey made in India showed that about 25 percent of the students who received their Master's degree from Lucknow University in arts, science, commerce and law between 1949 and 1953 were still unemployed in 1957. The survey also reported that about 47 percent of the liberal arts students, 51.4 percent of the science students, 7 percent of the commerce students, and 85.7 percent of the education students said they went to the university to get the necessary qualifications for government service. About 51 percent of the degree holders concluded that university education was a 'waste of time'. M Weiner, *Party Politics in India* (Princeton, 1957), pp8-10.

121 V Alba, 'The Middle Class Revolution', *New Politics* (New York), winter 1962, p71.

122 G D Overstreet and M Windmiller, *Communism in India* (Berkeley and Los Angeles, 1959), p540.

123 Ibid, p358.

124 G Kolko, *The Politics of War* (New York, 1968), p77.

125 Ibid, p77.

126 Ibid, p78.

127 I Birchall, *Bailing out the System* (London, 1986), pp39-40.

128 G Kolko, op cit, p95.

129 P Broué, 'The Italian Communist Party, the War and the Revolution', *Revolutionary History*, spring 1995, p111.

130 P Ginsburg, *A History of Contemporary Italy* (London, 1990), p22.

131 Ibid, p64.
132 Ibid, p68.
133 P Broué, op cit, p112.
134 P Ginsburg, op cit, pp42-43.
135 Ibid, p52.
136 This section on Germany is based upon part of the forthcoming book by Donny Gluckstein, *Barbarism: Nazi Counter-revolution, Capitalism and the Working Class* (London, 1999).
137 T Cliff, *Lenin: Revolution Besieged* (London, 1987), pp216-218.
138 T Cliff, *Trotsky: The Darker the Night the Brighter the Star*, op cit, p155.
139 Ibid, p286.
140 L Trotsky, *The Death Agony of Capitalism and the Tasks of the Fourth International* (London, 1980).
141 K Marx and F Engels, *Collected Works*, vol 11 (Moscow, 1979), p185. The reference is to Shakespeare, *Hamlet*, act 1, scene 5.

About the author

Tony Cliff is a founder member of the Socialist Workers Party in Britain. He was born in Palestine in 1917 and became a supporter of Leon Trotsky while still a teenager. His analysis of Russia as state capitalist was first formulated in the period after the Second World War in order to give the revolutionary left a more thorough analysis of the Russian and East European Stalinist states. 'The Class Nature of Stalinist Russia' was first distributed in duplicated form in 1948 and an amended version was first published as *Stalinist Russia: A Marxist Analysis* in 1955. A much larger version of this work, entitled *Russia: A Marxist Analysis,* was first published in 1964. A new edition of this book was then published in 1974 as *State Capitalism in Russia.* Cliff also published *Stalin's Satellites in Europe* in 1952 and this was followed by *Mao's China* in 1957.

Cliff's analysis insisted that the Stalinist regimes were not socialist but state capitalist since the state in these societies played the same role as that performed by the private capitalist firms and the state combined in Western capitalist societies. He predicted that increasing competition, in part through the arms race, would lead to renewed crises in the state capitalist societies.

As the long post-war boom began to subside in the late 1960s and early 1970s, heralding a renewal of the revolutionary left internationally as the student and workers' struggles of that period took shape, Cliff wrote two books relating closely to the class struggle in Britain. *Incomes Policy, Legislation and Shop Stewards,* co-authored with Colin Barker, was published in 1966 and *The Employers' Offensive: Productivity Deals and How to Fight Them* in 1970. The latter sold out of its initial print run of 10,000 in three weeks.

Cliff then began work on his three volume study of Lenin, in which he sought to recover the Marxist tradition on the crucial question of revolutionary organisation for a newly radicalised generation. This project was continued into the 1990s with a four volume study of Trotsky.

Tony Cliff's other publications include *Rosa Luxemburg*, first published in 1959, *Class Struggle and Women's Liberation* in 1984, and two books co-authored with Donny Gluckstein, *Marxism and Trade Union Struggle: The General Strike of 1926*, first published in 1986, and *The Labour Party: A Marxist History*, first published in 1988.

Principal works by Tony Cliff

Stalin's Satellites in Europe (London, 1952)
Stalinist Russia: A Marxist Analysis (London, 1955)
Mao's China (London, 1957)
Rosa Luxemburg (latest edition London, 1983)
Deflected Permanent Revolution (latest edition London, 1990)
Russia: A Marxist Analysis (London, 1964)
Incomes Policy, Legislation and Shop Stewards (London, 1966) with Colin Barker
The Employers' Offensive: Productivity Deals and How to Fight Them (London, 1970)
State Capitalism in Russia (latest edition London, 1996)
Neither Washington Nor Moscow: Essays on Revolutionary Socialism (London, 1982)
Class Struggle and Women's Liberation (London, 1984)
Marxism and Trade Union Struggle: The General Strike of 1926 (London, 1986) with Donny Gluckstein
Lenin: Volume 1, *Building the Party* (latest edition London, 1986)
Lenin: Volume 2, *All Power to the Soviets* (London, 1985)
Lenin: Volume 3, *The Revolution Besieged* (London, 1987)
The Labour Party: A Marxist History (latest edition London, 1994) with Donny Gluckstein
Trotsky: Volume 1, *Towards October* (London, 1989)
Trotsky: Volume 2, *Sword of the Revolution* (London, 1990)
Trotsky: Volume 3, *Fighting the Rising Stalinist Bureaucracy* (London, 1991)
Trotsky: Volume 4, *The Darker the Night the Brighter the Star* (London, 1993)

Index